IT'S TIME TO DUMP THE JUNK IN YOUR TRUNK!

YOUR JOURNEY INTO DEEP HEALING

EVERETT T. ROBINSON

DENVER, COLORADO

Foreword

This book is dedicated to Denise Aleeta Gail Robinson. Denise was my wife, best friend and spiritual mate for over forty-one years. She went home to be with Jesus on March 1, 2014, after a three year battle with ovarian cancer. She was sixty years old. She is the love of my life.

God gave Denise to me to be my helpmate in life because she was my opposite. Denise is best described by 1 Corinthians 13:4-6: she was patient, kind, unenvious, humble, never proud, never rude, not self-seeking, and not easily angered. She kept no record of wrongs done against her; she did not delight in evil and rejoiced in God's truth. I, on the other hand, am still working on improving in many of these areas.

A year before Denise realized she had cancer she started helping me teach the Deep Healing class at our church. Denise led the ladies small group (explained in the introduction). She loved it and understood how important it was for us to "help set the captives free" from the mental and emotional pain that all humans absorb during life's traumatic events. Denise understood life's pains, as she had them just like all the rest of us. I loved her term for these kinds of pains. She simply called them the "junk in her trunk."

Denise and I, and many loving brothers and sisters in the Lord, prayed that God would heal her on earth. Instead it was His will to "completely" heal her in heaven. Before she left this world, she told me she was happy to be going home and that she would be waiting for me there. She also told me to finish this book and get it published so others could be healed by Jesus, if not in this life, then when they get to heaven. God promises His children healing but does not tell us when, where or how it will happen. This book will help you develop the faith to accept that fact.

Denise leaving me was both the happiest and the most painful moment of my life. I was so happy she would never suffer pain again and was with Jesus, but I was also totally crushed that we would not be able to continue our journey through life together. This last year has been an emotional roller-coaster for me. It is only by God's Grace, and my following the healing principles taught in this book, that I have been able to stay sane. Scripture helps me as I struggle through every day.

Proverbs 3:5-6
Trust in the Lord with all your heart,
Lean not on your own understanding. In
all your ways acknowledge Him and He
will make your paths straight.

Surviving loss of a loved one is only one of the many deep pains in life that we need deep healing for, there are many, many others. Trust God and trust Denise that this information can heal you. If you allow God, He will remove "the junk in your trunk".

One of my fondest memories of Denise is her singing Praise songs to God; have fun singing up there Sweetie… I'll be home soon.

Acknowledgments

I wish to thank publicly the many people who supported my writing of this book. I am very grateful for the assistance I have received from each one of the following brothers and sisters in the Lord:

To Denise, the love of my life, I miss every minute that we helped others together in life, especially in this class. I really miss you knitting and smiling at me from the back of the room while I was talking up a storm. I am so glad you are with Jesus now, completely healed for eternity.

I want to give special thanks to Anne, Teri, and Mary who have stepped in to lead the ladies small groups now that Denise is with Jesus. God bless you Sisters.

I am also really blessed to have a daughter-in-law who paints and draws so well. Thanks Pam for doing the illustrations in the book, may God bless you for your kindness. Love you girl.

My deep appreciation goes out to Mary Olson for her extensive editing and formatting contributions; this book would never had been published without her. I also would like to thank Jeanette Littleton for her manuscript comments and formatting.

Many thanks, blessings and prayers for: Mary O., Bill B., Anne S., Lynn K., Teri R., Jackie S., David C., Joshua S., Dave Z., Menno F., Leann D., Phyllis F., Steve V., Mark D., Michelle D., Michelle H., Trish G., Paulette B., and Lance C.; all of whom were kind enough to write testimonies about the value of the healing information being presented to you in this book.

I am especially grateful for my brothers Bill, Robert, Mark and Josh for standing beside me and holding me up in prayer during some tough times this last year. Go Hawks!

I am indebted to Pastor Melonie, Jayne, Linda and all the other workers at Christ the King Community Church in Bellingham, WA for their support in providing valuable resources for the Deep Healing class mentioned within.

I also would like to thank Pastor Grant for teaching God's Word without compromise every week. Your humbleness before the Lord is always a bright light upon my pathway back home.

I wish to thank all the workers at Outskirts Press (Jamie and Lisa) for their patience, support, advice and energy in publishing this book.

Lastly, and most importantly, I am deeply and eternally grateful to Jesus Christ who made this all possible. Without HIS loving sacrifice and constant intercession for me with His Father, I'd still be crawling around outside in the darkness, whistling in the middle of this hurricane we call life.

Table of Contents

Introduction

Are You Ready and Willing to be Healed by God?

The Light of Scripture:

Hebrews 11:6
And without faith it is impossible to please God, because anyone who comes to him must believe that he exists and that he rewards those who <u>earnestly</u> seek him.

The Deep Healing Class taught by Everett and Denise Robinson was truly an answer to prayer for me. I had strayed from a lifetime of walking with the Lord and teaching others His truths. It was during this time of confusion in my life that I was desperately seeking guidance and answers to so many questions that brought me great sadness and depression. I had sought counsel from clergy and was prayed for, but was not given any tools to work through my "issues." It was through crying out to God for help that I was made aware of the Deep Healing Class.

The class was exactly what I needed! The lessons and spiritual guidance taught me why we are prone to sin and how God so wonderfully desires to bring us out of our "pit" and restore us to a relationship as His loved child. I learned how to come before God daily on my knees and hand over each and every problem to God, because "God has more healing than I have hurt."

I learned how to praise God in every situation, continually, every day. The material repeatedly taught me that God must be number one in my life. The tools I learned were invaluable to bring me to a place where God could minister to me and bring the much needed healing I so desperately desired.

I am so very thankful to Denise and Everett for sharing the gifts God has given them to touch the lives of so many hurting people. My relationship with God is richer because of it. Thanks so much!

Mary O.

You and your climbing guide are all set for the day. While parking the car in the lot at the beginning of the long trail up the summit, you feel motivated to make this climb. This is something you've always wanted to do, but just didn't have the time or energy to take it on. Getting married, raising kids, and working to earn a dollar always got in the way. But now this journey has become a top priority, and you are finally on the path!

At first, the walk through the woods is easy. The sun shines brightly as you leave the parking lot, but most of the trail is still in the shade of the thick, tall forest you are passing through. The air is cool and the pine trees smell wonderful! Small birds and squirrels dart through the undergrowth while you follow the guide up the trail. After an hour or two you begin a steeper climb, leaving the forest behind.

The smooth trail you were walking on has now turned to hard rock, as you begin moving up the face of the mountain. The backpack that was once light and secure on your back now feels twice as heavy. Moving up the incline you realize the guide is farther ahead of you and you are breathing much heavier now. Without the shade from the trees, the sun speaks to you in harsher tones than before. Glancing at your watch, you realize time has moved faster than you thought. You are nowhere near where you thought you would be at this time in your climb. You have so much farther to go.

Still, you are excited about your journey. The possibilities of learning new things about yourself give you extra strength to keep moving up the steep rock face. *This is all good exercise,* you think, and you are determined to handle the workload no matter what. Sweat is now streaming off your face and you are starting to wonder where your guide is. You can no longer see him.

As you move upwards, the pull of gravity upon your body is getting heavier. Each step is a reminder of the weight of your backpack. After another hour of steady climbing, you crawl over a ledge onto a small flat spot just big enough to lie down on. Your legs and your back ache as you try to get comfortable. Totally soaked in sweat and breathing heavily, you can't relax with the pack on your back. So slowly and carefully you take it off, set it next to you, and lean against it.

Looking down to where you started, you are amazed just how high up you are. The first thought of quitting goes through your mind. Your legs throb and your heart pounds. Fear enters your mind and the thought, *What if I can't make it?* passes through your brain.

Unexpectedly you sense your guide next to you. His face is calm and peaceful. You are so happy he is back. You are not alone.

Pointing to your pack your guide asks, "What is there in the pack that is so important you can't get rid of it?"

Stunned by the question you suddenly notice his pack is small compared to yours.

"Everything in my pack is absolutely necessary," you quickly reply back. "Open it up, and let's take a look at what's in it," he demands.

Surprised you stammer, "I only carry things that are valuable, things I must have."

"Open it up. Let's see what's so valuable that you let it keep you from finishing your journey," your guide replies.

Every inch of your mind tells you not to open the pack, after all it's your stuff and he has no right to see what's inside. But you know he is right, so you reluctantly obey his command.

Unpacking Your Stuff

As you open the pack, your guide reaches in and takes the first thing off the top. Amazingly it's a rock! Watching your guide examine it you think, "*How did that get in there?*"

"This seems to be pretty useless; is there a reason you're carrying it around with you?" he asks.

"Not really, I don't even remember where I picked it up," you reply weakly.

"Do you know what kind of rock this is?"

"Nooooo," you stutter, "do they have names?"

"This one is very common, it is called Pride. Shall I throw it away" he asks as he tosses it over the cliff? He reaches into your bag to pull out another rock that is even bigger than the first one.

"Oh yes, here is one you definitely need to let go of, it's called Worry. And this one is Loneliness, here is Grief and this one is Bitterness. Wow, I thought I would find this one in here…Self-Centeredness…it is always close to the others."

Stunned, you sit there as he pulls one rock out after another naming each one as he piles them on the edge of the ledge. Soon the pile is so big there is no room for more rocks. You feel embarrassed and even humiliated knowing there is nothing of value in your pack. The rocks are only "dead weight" you've been hauling up the mountain. Anger surges through you for being so dumb and thinking your "stuff" was valuable and essential for your life's journey.

In a rage, you suddenly push all the rocks over the ledge. You cannot look your guide in the eye. Your head is down and you feel ashamed of what he saw in your pack. You suddenly feel a strong impulse to stand up and jump over the edge as well, but just before you can do so your guide speaks.

"I remember the first trip in my journey," he says. "We were just about here when my guide had me unpack my 'stuff.' I had way more rocks than you did, and the last one was huge!"

Surprised at his response you weakly ask, "What was it?"

"Self-condemnation," he replies. "If I were you, I would make sure your pack is completely empty."

Opening up your pack once more you notice one very large rock still at the bottom of your bag. As you take it out, you realize it weighs much more than any one of the others. Without asking, you know deep down inside of you its name is Self-hatred. Placing it on the ledge you turn to your guide and ask, "What do you want me to do with it?"

"Time to kick it over the edge, only you can do it—kick it over or put it back in your bag and we will climb some more," he responds as he stands up.

"No," you yell loudly swiftly pushing it off the edge. *Crash! Bam! Boom!* It makes loud sounds rolling down the hill through the thick brush.

Your guide smiles and says it's time to go, as he begins walking back down the trail you just came up.

Quickly getting to your feet you ask him, "Where are you going? Aren't we going to finish the climb?"

He looks up at you on the ledge and says, "We didn't come to finish the climb. Conquering mountains is all about proving you are someone you really aren't. Reaching the top of the mountain was never part of your plan for healing. We came just far enough for you to unload the contamination that was in you. Now that you have done that, we can continue with the next part of your journey which awaits you back where you first started."

Moving quickly off the ledge and back onto the trail, you realize the journey is so much easier now than it was when you were heading in the wrong direction and carrying all that self-destructive weight. A new sense of hope and urgency replaces your rocks motivating you toward the rest of your journey.

What is Deep Healing?

Healing is a term that can include many human conditions and situations. In this book, we focus primarily on "Deep Healing" within your personality and spirit rather than physical, marital, or financial healing. Although, much of the information provided to you can help in those areas as well. Deep Healing is also sometimes referred to as "Inner Healing".

Deep Healing is the restorative act of the Holy Spirit within you that returns your mind, heart, and life to where God intends them to be.

For the purpose of your "Deep Healing," we will ask God to heal (if you need healing) five things in you:

1. Your spiritual relationship and walk with Him.
2. The worldly corruption that has collected in your mind.
3. The hardness in your heart caused by loss and/or abuse.
4. The dysfunctional and unloving ways you now relate to yourself.
5. The dysfunctional and unloving ways you now relate to others.

Healing Doesn't Mean Forgetting

When I was eleven years old, I was playing catch with my older brother John. We were in an old vacant lot that had more weeds and dirt mounds than grass, but it was large and right next to our house. After many throws, John threw the baseball high and off to my right side.
Running sideways to catch the ball I tripped over what appeared to be a large dirt mound. I went down face first and was stunned. As I laid there I thought to myself, "What in the world did I trip over?"

Before I could get up, I heard my mom yelling at us from the house. John came running over right away and said, "Get up to the house, quick." I said, "I'm okay, I just want to find my baseball." He then grabbed my left arm and held it up in front of my face. My left arm was very bloody and the blood was dripping all over the ground. I could see a deep gash in my forearm, but couldn't feel my arm from the elbow down. Later I found out that the mound was really an old upside down car trunk lid that was covered over by high weeds. The lid had one very jagged piece of metal sticking up and I hit it with my left arm when I went down.

I was then taken to the doctor's office where I received a shot and 30 stitches. The strange thing is that I didn't feel anything. The doctor told my mom that time would tell if I would ever be able to use my left arm and hand again, because the cut went all the way to the bone. Praise God my arm was back working within the week and I have never had any problems with it since.

The moral of the story is that when we experience a traumatic event we often are so shocked we don't really understand how bad we have been hurt. Our minds tend to suppress the incident, so we can "cope" with what is happening in the moment.

During the rest of my life, I never thought much about what had happened, or how I could have ended up, except when I looked at my arm and see my scar. The minute I see it or touch it I am immediately transformed back to the dirty lot, my bloody arm and the doctor's office. I have not forgotten it and am very grateful that it does not take energy away from me, which is another important point of the story.

Every Personality Rock Creates an Emotional Energy Drain

Anytime you are traumatized by people or events during your lifetime, you receive an "emotional scar" that runs deep within your personality. When a traumatic experience goes unhealed, it sucks energy from your personality which is trying to keep it suppressed. While it seems to be lying dormant, sooner or later it gets triggered by words, similar experiences or other traumatic events happening to you or someone else. Each time it comes up and you don't go through a healing process, you end up suppressing it again which takes more energy, because you are trying to keep it hidden within your personality.

When you have many unhealed "emotional scars", you lose so much energy you often feel tired, afraid and depressed. You begin looking for and using anything that will give you a boost of energy. These things are called "uppers" and include actions such as: binge eating, drinking sugar filled soft drinks, taking wild and dangerous risks, excessive shopping, excessive alcohol and/or drug consumption, sexual experimentation, high risk acts and relationships with people you think can and will "rescue" you with their energy which they cannot do.

Our avoiding healing just compounds our trauma and pain. We often think, "I will never, ever forget what happened to me." The healing process does not require that you forget what happened; just that you forgive others, yourself and let God heal your inner pain through His love. This is not easy and it does not guarantee you won't experience new traumas. It does however teach us a process we can use when the next trauma happens (and it is just around the corner). The grief cycle and healing process will be discussed in greater depth later in the book.

I pray that you will read every lesson with anticipation and gratefulness for the many healing truths that God will give you. Here comes one now!

Healing Truth No. 1
The truth will set you free.

The concepts in this book only work if you accept Jesus as your Lord. Everything presented in this book is based on the fact that Jesus not only died so you can be free from your sins (pain), but that Jesus also sits at the right hand of your Father in heaven so you can be healed. Through your relationship with Jesus, you gain access to God's truth about living and being healed.

> **John 8:31-32**
> *To the Jews who had believed him, Jesus said, "If you hold to my teaching, you are really my disciples. Then you will know the truth, and the truth will set you free."*

Healing Truth No. 2
God has more healing than you have "Personality Rocks."

I learned a long time ago that healing can be "for better or for worse;" going half way most often just increases the pain that haunts us. Freedom from suffering lies in the complete surrender of your life to God's will. Doing this is impossible without God's help, without His power.

This book acts like a "road sign" pointing you toward God's gift of healing. I am simply a messenger sent to focus you on key areas of your personality that God wants to restore. As you work though each lesson activity, please take time to pray and write down what God shows you.

Healing Truth No. 3
Deep spiritual healing requires God's light.

Many of the wounds you have received during your life have been caused by other people, but many have also come from bad choices you have made trying to please others and yourself. You thought you were smart and in-control enough to make safe decisions, but they just put you in pain and sadness. For example, acquiring excessive debt is just one instance of how people wound themselves, thinking they know what is financially best for their lives.

These intense wounds not only create great pain in your life, but much worse they redirect the purpose God created you for. When sidetracked by your agony, you often move deeper into the darkness God warned you to stay away from. This book has been created to assist you with your journey back home . . . back into God's healing light.

> **1 John 1:5-7**
> *This is the message we have heard from him and declare to you: God is light; in him there is no darkness at all. If we claim to have fellowship with him yet walk in the darkness, we lie and do not live by the truth. But if we walk in the light, as he is in the light, we have fellowship with one another, and the blood of Jesus, his Son, purifies us from all sin.*

Healing Truth No. 4
Your healing is your responsibility.

Healing is such a stunning promise from God that it may scare you off. You habitually think you can never accomplish it. Your mind repeatedly tells you, "While others may find healing and inner peace, I never will."

This lie and many others will be exposed *if* you choose to personalize the truths this teaching will provide to you. ***The success of your healing totally depends on your full participation. No one else can take these steps for you.*** Passive resistance in the form of listening to "predetermined mental lies" without challenging yourself to move forward by faith, will only keep you stuck in your suffering.

No one can make you be healed, if you do not want to be. God gives every person free will to choose Him or to live apart from Him. If you choose God, you will still suffer in life (yes Christians get sick, and are persecuted, and all of us physically die), but you will not suffer as much as when you choose to live without Him. While Jesus suffered during His life on earth, He still praised God and chose God's will for His life.

Hebrews 5:7-9
During the days of Jesus' life on earth, he offered up prayers and petitions with fervent cries and tears to the one who could save him from death, and he was heard because of his reverent submission. Although he was a son, he learned obedience from what he suffered and, once made perfect, he became the source of eternal salvation for all who obey him . . .

Healing Truth No. 5
The amount of time you spend praying, learning God's word and surrendering your need to control your life will determine how fast you will be healed.

Your healing will come as you submit to God in Jesus' name, also as you chose to let God's Word change your mind and your heart.

Psalm 119:105
Your Word is a lamp to my feet and a light to my path.

Deep Healing is designed to be a personal challenge. It was created to be a full participation workbook for those who truly seek healing. Healing, like climbing the mountain of pain you have in your life, requires effort. Those who sit, listen and simply read the book, but refuse to allow God to remove the "rocks" from their personality, will gain little from the healing process. Those who seek God while completing the activities provided will be more than blessed with His loving touch.

Are You Ready and Willing to be Healed?

Few people get healed by hiding in the audience. You will find healing as you fully participate in the work that is provided within each lesson. I like to use a simple classification system to show you four possible ways people tend to approach learning. See if you can identify which one you are.

Level 1 Learners –

These individuals are not ready or willing to learn or change one thing in their personality or lives. They tend to have major trust and anger issues which are indicated by their constant complaining and blaming of others. They have too much "pride in their stride" to let others show them how to find God's healing and freedom in Christ. They are "spiritually stubborn" and refuse God's love.

Level 2 Learners -

These people are ready and willing to "think and talk" about changing the negativity in their lives, but never do follow through. They like sitting in the audience asking questions, but they rarely hear and apply the answers. They lack faith to believe God really cares about them and are ruled by fear and worry. They often come close to the healing line, but seldom step across it.

Level 3 Learners -

These individuals have as many issues as Level 1 and 2 learners, but they have come to the realization that God is the only way. They know they have wasted too much time in their lives living in defeat and are now crossing the line to receive their healing. They are ready and willing to learn, fail and trust God again and again to receive healing and positive change in their life.

Level 4 Learners –

These are men and women who live at Level 3 daily so they can complete their purpose in life, which is helping others make it to level 3 and freedom. They understand and live by the principle that if they have freely received God's mercies they must also freely give God's mercies to others. In God's Kingdom, we have to give God's love away to keep receiving it.

To illustrate this Spiritual progression called growth, here is a poem written by my friend Bill. He sent it to me during the first year of his five-year prison sentence.

Wasted Time

The time that I've wasted is my biggest regret
Spent in these places I'll never forget,
Sitting, thinking of things that I've done
The crying, the laughing, the hurt and the fun.

Now it's just me; the shame and the guilt
Behind a wall of emptiness I alone have built,
I'm trapped in my body, just wanting to run
Back to my youth with its laughter and fun.

The chase is over, there's no place to hide
Everything is gone, including the pride,
With reality staring me right in the face I'm
scared, alone, and stuck in this place

Memories of the past flash through my head
The pain is obvious by the tears that I shed,
I ask myself, "Why…where did I go wrong?"
I guess I was weak when I should have been strong.

Life in the fast lane, on seeds I have sown
My feelings were lost, afraid to be shown,
As I look at my past it's so easy to see
The fear that I had; afraid to be me.

Now I wait for the day I'll get a new start
And the dreams I still hold in my heart,
I know I can make it, at least I must try
Cause I've so much to live for and I don't want to die.

Bill B.

Testimonies from Brothers and Sisters Receiving God's Healing

In the Introduction and at the beginning of the each lesson I have added testimonies from men and women that have finished the Deep Healing class. Many of them started off in fear, confusion, and anger like some of you may be doing. As you read their letters, you will "hear" just how important this healing information was in their finding freedom from their life's pain.

Here is Bill B's testimony after God healed him by taking him through the 4 learning levels. He now ministers to men who are in prison. He spends a tremendous amount of time writing them, going to see them in person and assisting them to relocate and get reestablished after they have finished their sentences. He let God move him from being a victim to being God's Servant. He let God lead him to his purpose.

Living so many years of my life just for me and doing things my way was not working for me. My life was destructive and hurtful for myself and others. These destructive patterns eventually led me to years in an 8 x 10 cell. For a long time I thought I could fix myself but I could not do any of this on my own. It was during this time when I met God face to face that my healing began. With this healing I found that life was worth living. I still am learning how to truly love and to live the life God created for me to live.

Having been released from a physical prison of bars and razor wire I came to realize that one does not have to be "locked up" to be in prison. I needed to be "Plugged in", connected to God's power, outside of those bars as much as I did inside. I also needed others and the tools available to help me become a man of God.

Taking the class Everett teaches helped me more than I can say. In this class I learned many things that keep me sober and moving straight towards God. One was how plugging in to God every morning is vital to my daily walk. I also learned that my negative inner voice was setting me up to fail and how I could change my negative thoughts and feelings into loving statements towards me.

Another valuable lesson was how my past "Trails of Shame" were still pulling me down spiritually. In class I found very useful information and solutions for leaving these trails behind. And being challenged in class to be honest and "transparent" about my struggles and weaknesses with other men who have similar issues has really helped me to trust again. Trust God, trust others but more importantly, to trust me.

I am really looking forward to using the many things God has taught me through this class to help other men who are on the same journey of recovery that I am on. It is now my purpose for living. I can't wait to get copies of this book as I know so many men who need direction and support.

Bill B.

Here is a clear testimony from Anne who took several classes and then became a ladies small group leader.

Recovery by definition means returning to a normal state of health, mind and strength. To me it means that and so much more. After four years of sharing, crying and rejoicing in the healing that recovery classes bring I can now confidently say out loud that "I Matter" and that I like who I am becoming.

I am inspired by those, like my friends and teachers Denise and Everett, who reached out and helped me on my journey when I felt I was going through everything alone. I learned so much by taking the class and reviewing the manuscript for this book. I only wished I had read it when I was younger then I would not have been so hard on myself and others.

I am blessed and encouraged by the tremendous support of those who heard my stories and understood. I am excited to move forward and celebrate my life knowing that God and recovery has saved it.

Anne S.

A Small Group Testimony

When small group guidelines are put in place and followed, then trust, sharing and personal healing greatly increase as indicated by the following testimony.

I took this class because it was recommended to me by a friend. It's like none other I have ever taken. Everett has many meaningful and key phrases to remind us how to conquer our flesh. We either control our flesh or it controls us. He has given us several tools to transform our self-image, change our inner voice, and become more intimate with Jesus. These tools will benefit me as I continue to use them long after the class has ended.

I was very impressed with how vulnerable and honest the gals were in my group. We grew to truly care for one another thru sharing and prayer. Teri did a great job leading.

We're all broken people, we have dysfunction in our lives, we have been hurt and we have hurt others. This class is a journey into my healing so that I can become who God has planned for me to be and I, in turn, can glorify Him.

Thank you Everett for your ministry and for openly sharing your journey with us!

Sincerely,

Lynn K.

Small Group Guidelines (if using small groups in a class format)

If possible, I highly recommend using this book in a two-hour class situation that includes at least forty-five minutes to an hour for small group sharing and prayer. Men are in male-only groups with a male leader; women are in women-only groups with a female leader.

For small groups to work effectively, guidelines need to be introduced from the beginning and maintained throughout the class. Here are the guidelines that I use to structure group interaction and provide safety for all who participate:

1. Confidentiality is very important. What is shared in the class or small group stays in the class or small group. Telling outsiders (even while praying) what you heard group members say will not help you or the people who shared the information. Trust is required for others to work on their issues, so please honor what others share in confidence.

2. Group is a time and place to discuss or confess your inner experiences, not to <u>complain</u> about what others have done to you. The focus of your sharing should be on *your* behavior, feelings, thoughts, and fears about your recovery. You can share things from your inventory activities or talk about insights you had while listening to the class lesson.

3. Group time is valuable and not long enough to tell your complete life story so be "short and specific." It is not necessary or helpful to go into great detail about how you were hurt or how often; instead, briefly share what the problem is and how it is affecting you right now.

> **Unacceptable**: "My dad was a no-good drunk who (ten minutes later you are still talking about your dad's character flaws).

> **Acceptable**: "My dad was a drunk who verbally hurt everyone in my family. I realize now that I am still afraid of critical people, and I constantly criticize myself!"

4. Tell your story and discuss your problems using "I" statements.

> **Unacceptable:** "My wife is so critical and unloving, she's always . . ."

> **Acceptable:** "I want to stop remembering what my first boss did to me."

5. Take ownership for your pain and recovery. Blaming others is not healthy and does not help you recover. Talking about how others contributed to your "pain-in" and "pain-out" is acceptable only if you do not blame people for your choices in life.

6. Talking about a person's relationship to you (my boss, my dad, etc.) is acceptable but naming people ("My boss, Bill Brown, said to me . . .") is not acceptable.

7. No Cross Talking. Group members are not allowed to ask questions about what others are sharing in group. Group leaders are the only people in the group who can ask questions or direct (limit) someone's sharing.

Asking questions reflects your need to know, not their need to tell. It also uses up valuable group time and stops deeper sharing from occurring. Giving advice is also not acceptable. It reveals your need to "fix" someone rather than letting God fix them. It might also indicate that you have a codependency issue which is a topic we will cover later in this book.

8. Do not interrupt others while they are sharing in group. One person shares at a time. Do not comment on what you "think" while they are talking, and no preaching or teaching is allowed. Look at the speaker while he or she is talking; this is respectful. Be open to learning from what is being shared. It might be something you also need to work on.

9. Group leaders are the only ones responsible to keep the group on track. Group leaders have the right to stop discussion if they think a member is taking too long or is "off base" in his or her conversation. If you have issues with a group leader, please talk with your class instructor about it.

10. No profanity (rude and crude talk or jokes) is allowed in class or in small group. The group is seeking God's blessings, and other people have the right to not hear "garbage" coming out of someone's mouth.

11. Protecting everyone in the group is a top priority, so coming to class or group under the influence of alcohol or drugs is unacceptable. If you are in such a condition, do not come to class or group until you have stopped using and finished going through withdrawals (at least a 60-day sobriety is a good rule of thumb).

Prayer Requests (sample form used only in small group setting)

Please write down the first name of each person in your group and his or her weekly prayer requests. Prayer requests should focus on your healing issues *that are lesson related,* not other people's issues, such as getting a pay raise at work, relatives who are sick, etc.

Pray for each person in your group every day during the next week. You must maintain confidentiality. These prayers are not to be shared with people outside of your group. When the week is finished, destroy each prayer sheet. Do not leave them lying around for others to read.

Each request should be short and to the point. God knows all the details of your life and problems', so writing out more than a full sentence is not necessary.

Example: I need prayer this week for strength to read my Bible every day instead of reading other things that are polluting my mind.

A good focusing question to ask everyone is, "How can we pray for <u>you</u> this week?"

<u>First Name</u>　　　　　<u>Prayer Request</u>

1.

2.

3.

4.

5.

6.

7.

8.

9.

Deep Healing: Section One
Your Flesh is Not Your Friend!

The Light of Scripture:

2 Peter 1: 2-4
Grace and peace be yours in abundance through the knowledge of God and of Jesus our Lord.

His divine <u>power</u> has given us everything we need for life and godliness through our knowledge of him who called us by his own glory and goodness.

Through these he has given us his very great and precious promises, so that through them you may participate in the divine nature and escape the corruption in the world caused by evil desires.

A Testimony to God's Deep Healing

Hallelujah and praise God for taking me through this Deep Healing journey.

I am 54 years old and spent the last 14 years seeking healing from childhood and adulthood wounds. I did this through several different therapists and through conventional counseling methods, with no success.

I took this class the first time and was barely feeling the effects of those heavy rocks being removed from my pack. After attending the second time, I can honestly say I no longer experience the pain and hurt. With God's blessing and grace, I was freed of the horrible bondage my past put me through. I am a stronger, more confident person who is able to trust and believe in all the wonderful gifts God has for us.

I am forever grateful and will continue to stay "plugged in" and "praise God (PG10X)" every day! I have also learned how to disregard that "negative inner voice," and to be mindful that "my flesh is not my friend."

God bless Everett and Denise for being the messengers. Their ministry has more value than words could ever begin to express. My gratitude is immense and I pray they continue to touch and comfort others who are struggling with deep emotional wounds.

Teri R.

Deep Healing: Lesson One

Plugging-In to God's Power

The Light of Scripture:

> **Psalm 30:2**
> *O Lord my God, I called to you for help and you healed me.*

A Testimony to God's Deep Healing

Relief! I have finally found Relief! One evening I discovered just how trapped in my mind, in my "stinking thinking" I was. In a moment I realized just how poorly I had valued myself daily my whole life. I believed all the lies in my inner voice was telling me and finally understood how trapped I was inside my own thoughts.

When I was recording my self-worth inventory I could see just how negative all the lies in my inner voice really were. How those thoughts were destroying me and all that I loved. But I soon discovered empowerment as God handed me a roadmap for healing my mind. The joy I felt when I discovered that I wasn't a misfit, that God didn't want to destroy me...that he loved me. My stronghold of fear-my oldest and cleverest foe-was loosened. Somehow, the truth of God not sparing his Son Jesus for my sake rescued me from all the lies...from Satan's lies that repeatedly told me that God did not really want me. But God's perfect love drove out my fear and I now know that I can have success from addiction.

On that evening I also found out how to read the roadmap to healing through learning about specific and identifiable prayer. What drove me to control my external environment was fear. So now I pray, "Father in Heaven, please remove this fear from me." Sometimes I ask God to, "Hold my hand while we both walk down this road of fear together." I am so strengthened when God is holding my hand and encouraged when He carries me along the path I am now walking. God's love strikes at the core of my fear and renders it powerless in my life. The truth has set me free.

It is amazing how in one evening, while taking inventory of my self-worth, self-concept and negative inner voice, the Truth got ahold of my insides and I experienced freedom from addiction by surrendering my flesh to my Father in Heaven in Jesus name. I now have hope where I once had anxiety, love where I once had anger and faith where I once had fear. Praise Jesus!

David C.

Will You Receive and Use God's Gifts?

Romans 6:22-23
But now that you have been set free from sin and have become slaves to God, the benefit you reap leads to holiness, and the result is eternal life. For the wages of sin is death, but the gift of God is eternal life in Christ Jesus our Lord.

Gift One: Healing that brings Freedom, Holiness, and Eternal Life

I imagine an enormous room filled with people, and before them, under a very large cross, are many nicely wrapped presents, gifts from God! Jesus is standing at the foot of the cross calling each person to come up and receive a present with his or her name on it. Sitting there, I am awestruck as I stare at Jesus.

As I wait for my name to be called, I notice that some people do not go to Him when He calls them. They don't believe He is who He says He is, and they want nothing to do with Him.
Others do not go up because they don't believe He really has a present with their name on it.
And still others do not go up because they think the packages hold nothing of value.
Selfishly, others tell Jesus to bring the gifts to them because they are too busy to go up and receive their gift.

Then I notice someone go and take a gift from Jesus, but when he returns to his place he doesn't open it. He just sets it under his chair. Another person goes up and receives her gift and opens it immediately upon returning to her spot. But when she sees what's inside, she tosses it aside to play with things she thinks are more entertaining. Another person receives their gift and immediately turns and gives it to someone else and then sits back down.

I was shocked when I heard Jesus call my name. I was so up in my head watching the others that I was not ready. My heart raced as I stumbled up to get my present. Before I touched it I looked at Jesus and said, "Thank you for what you are giving me."

Jesus smiled, put the present down and said, "You may go, your faith has healed you."

At that moment, I realized that Jesus was God's greatest gift. Suddenly I was outside the room telling others about the gifts that God wanted to give them.

What will you do with the gifts God has for you? Will you accept and use them by faith and be healed? Every day you must choose to follow Jesus by using your gifts to help others, even when it is not entertaining or prosperous to do so.

Healing Truth No. 6
God's presents are only valuable, if you accept them and use them now--today.

> *"Yesterday is history, tomorrow is a mystery, and today*
> *is a gift; that's why they call it the present."*
> **Eleanor Roosevelt**

Gift Two: God Wants to Put His Power into Our Inner Beings

Most of us have cell phones, which are fascinating and useful tools when they work correctly. Yet with all their many functions and features, cell phones are useless when the battery dies. This is why every night we plug them into a power source, so the battery is recharged for the next day.

Believe it or not, God created us just like cell phones. We have memory, talk with others, text messages to ourselves through our thinking, take and view pictures inside our minds; and most importantly we have a battery, our human spirit, that needs charging.

When your spirit is not plugged into God's Spirit on a daily basis, you soon stop functioning as you were designed to. You lose power and become weak. In short, you lack the power to do the daily tasks God requires you to do.

For instance, loving other people often drains our battery more than it charges it. The deep pain within us alters our positive energy into negative energy. Instead of becoming a giver as God intended, we become takers. This occurs when we unsuccessfully attempt to recharge our spirits through human relationships and activities, rather than by plugging into the Holy Spirit. Healing comes only when God's power flows through us every day.

Healing Truth No. 7 - Removing pain requires God's power entering into your inner being.

Ephesians 3:16

*For this reason I **kneel before the Father,** from whom his whole family in heaven and on earth derives its name. I pray that out of his glorious riches he may strengthen you **with power through his Spirit in your inner being.***

So How Do You Receive God's Power in Your Inner Being?

1. To stand firm in the world, you must first kneel before God daily.

2. Deny yourself (sinful nature), take up your cross, and follow Jesus every day.

   Luke 9:23
   And he said to all, "If anyone would come after me, let him deny himself and take up his cross daily and follow me."

3. To follow Jesus every day takes Spirit Power. To receive God's power, you must be connected (plugged in) to Jesus who is God's vine.

   John 15:5
   I am the vine; you are the branches. If a man remains in me and I in him, he will bear much fruit; apart from me you can do nothing.

Another great illustration of plugging-in is using power tools. Like a power tool, you were created to function for a purpose. Each tool is highly beneficial, when connected to a power source. While not every person is the same, we all must rely on the same power, if we want to function as we were created to perform. When we are unplugged, we are of little use.

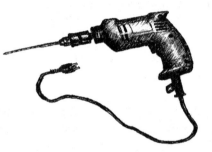

Healing Truth No. 8
God gave you a short cord and a small battery, so you have to stay close to Him. Disconnected from God you only harm yourself and others.

How Do You Get Plugged-in to God's Power?

1. Praise God (PG10X) ten times for all things. Rejoice in the Lord always.
2. Always pray in the name of Jesus.
3. Pray by Faith, not by fear.
4. Talk to God about people before you talk to people about God.
5. Confess self-hatred as sin.
6. Read and memorize scripture verses.
7. Worship, fellowship and study the bible with other believers.
8. Listen to and sing songs of praise to God.
9. Humble yourself before the Lord Jesus and He will lift you up.
10. Testify to others about what God is doing in your life.
11. Pray more for others needs than you pray for your own.
12. Ask God for a daily appointment, a time to kneel before your King. To be plugged in, you must meet God every day at the cross to receive His grace (power) to live.

Jesus is our example. We must be like Christ, if we are to follow Him. If He got up early and "plugged in" to the Holy Spirit, then we should do no less.

> **Mark 1:35**
> *Very early in the morning, while it was still dark, Jesus got up, left the house and went off to a solitary place, where he prayed.*

Gift Three: God's Power "Protects" Us from Our Enemies

God's Holy Spirit and power consists of: love, grace, forgiveness, wisdom, healing, holiness, and energy to obey His commands. You cannot humanly succeed at fulfilling God's commands without His power. The Holy Spirit also provides you with the protection you need to not be deceived and destroyed by your three biggest enemies.

The Bible identifies three major enemies you (we) must face: Satan, the world, and your own flesh (sinful nature), which works with the first two enemies to harm you and others.

Each of these adversaries cause great pain during your lifetime, and each are much more powerful than you. To protect yourself from the daily attacks, you need a power greater than they are. You need the power of the Holy Spirit. When you are "plugged in", God gives you:

1. Power to "Stand Firm" against the enemy inside of you. Your sinful nature, self, flesh, inappropriate thoughts, evil desires, etc.

2. Power to "Stand Firm" against the enemy you see all around you. The world: everything that exists outside of your body, flesh, and personality. This includes everyone else's flesh.

3. Power to "Stand Firm" against the enemy you cannot see. Satan, demons, evil spirits, powers and principalities in the heavenly realms, etc.

This book is written to help you win the war with enemy number one which is your flesh, sinful human nature. This does not mean the other two are not just as important. Very briefly let me say that spiritual warfare is very real and goes on around you 24 hours a day, all around the world. God promises you protection from the evil one (John 17:14-15; 1 Peter 5:8-9). Scripture also states that God does not want you to become polluted by the world (James 1:27) or to become friends with the world (James 4:4). And of course, God wants you to have control over yourself (flesh) so you can pray (1 Peter 4:7). I hope to write another book to address many of the key healing issues with the enemies outside your flesh.

> With God's Power guiding you,
> your Journey into Deep Healing
> will be a blessing
> rather than a curse.

Gift Four: God Provides Steps for Spiritual Success

Plugging into Jesus' power (the Holy Spirit) gives you a chance to stand firm against your flesh, the world, and Satan. To be victorious God has given you spiritual steps to follow:

1. **Surrender** your will daily in Jesus' name.

Agree with God that His Will is better for your healing than your will. Agree that Jesus died for your sins, washing them away with His loving sacrifice on the cross, so that your soul and spirit might be washed clean. Take up your cross daily by "plugging into" His Holy Spirit through praise, prayer, reading and memorizing His Word.

2. **Submit** to God's will.

Surrender your will to God, for His will for your life. Obey His commands, so you are trained for the good works He has already created for you to do. Participate in God's "Spiritual Boot Camp", so you will be strong enough to make the sacrifices that He will ask of you.

3. **Sacrifice** everything that is keeping you from Submitting and Serving God and others.

Let God strip away all of the character flaws, relationships, plans, goals, things, and commitments that get between you and the purpose He has created you to accomplish.

4. **Serve** others through God's Grace (love, mercy, patience, wisdom, and power).

Fulfill your Christian ministry by putting others spiritual (eternal) welfare before your earthly safety and comfort.

5. **Stand Firm** in God's Power.

Focus on the first four steps daily so when evil comes against you it does not prevail or sidetrack you from God's purpose for your life. Be ready to always give your testimony for Jesus, no matter what the forces against you might be. Learn to work and rest in God's grace.

A Quick Reality Check

You can find where your current spiritual development is by reviewing the steps listed above in reverse order as presented below:

- If you are not **standing firm**, you know that you are not serving in God's power.
- If you are not **serving** in God's power, you know you are not sacrificing something God requires from you.
- If you are not **sacrificing** something God requires, you know that you are not fully in submission to Him.
- If you are not fully in **submission** to Him, you know you have not totally surrendered your life (will, mind, heart) to Jesus.
- If you have not **surrendered** your heart to Jesus, now is the time to do so.

Pray for God's Free Gift of Salvation

Salvation is a gift from God, it cannot be earned by works or good deeds, we all must ask for it and receive it by Faith (read all of Ephesians Chapter 2). God's love, in giving us forgiveness and His Holy Spirit cleans us from all past mistakes. I love Titus 3:3-5 and often personalize it when reading it. For instance, "At one time I too was foolish, disobedient, deceived,"

Titus 3:3-5

At one time we too were foolish, disobedient, deceived and enslaved by all kinds of passions and pleasures. We lived in malice and envy, being hated and hating one another. But when the kindness and love of God our Savior appeared, he saved us, not because of righteous things we had done, but because of his mercy. He saved us through the washing of rebirth and renewal by the Holy Spirit, whom he poured out on us generously through Jesus Christ our Savior, so that, having been justified by his grace, we might become heirs having the hope of eternal life.

If you have not already asked God for His greatest gift, below is a simple prayer of salvation. You can use this prayer to ask God to help you surrender your will to Him, so you can repent and be saved. The words are not as important as is the level of your willingness to let God heal you.

"Dear Father in Heaven, please help me. I surrender my life and my will to you in Jesus' name. I believe that Jesus died for my sins and I repent of (name anything that God brings into your mind) and ask for your power to pray every day. Thank you for your love for me. Please help me be more like you and less like me."

Healing Truth No. 9
Your flesh is not your friend; in fact, it is your worst enemy. You believe it is "on your side", when it is working very hard every day to harm you.

Eight Key Things That Will "Unplug" You from God's Power

Staying plugged into God's power can only happened, if we pray and surrender our will for our lives daily. Our flesh does not want us doing that, so it attacks us from within to unplug us from His power. Here are a few ways that our flesh disconnects us from the help we need:

1. Toxic Thoughts (negative inner voice, ungodly fantasies, denial)
2. Freaky Fears (worry, anxiety, paranoia, phobias, insecurities)
3. Emergency Emotions (reactive feelings that occur during stress, crisis)
4. Destructive Decisions (impulsive decision making that causes harm)
5. Belligerent Behaviors (lying, gossiping, mocking, quarreling, sarcasm, etc.)
6. Caustic Criticism (attacking personalities as well as behaviors)
7. Reoccurring Rocky Relationships (repeatedly being attracted to and picking the same negative patterns in other people you bond with)
8. Misguided Morals (seeking what feels good rather than pursuing what is right before God)

1 Corinthians 15: 50
I declare to you, brothers, that flesh and blood cannot inherit the kingdom of God, nor does the perishable inherit the imperishable.

For the purpose of teaching this truth, the definition of "flesh" includes: "sinful nature," "body," and "self." The flesh contains our: wills, minds, hearts, desires, needs, fears, and parts of the body such as eyes, hands, feet, etc. It includes all of our thoughts, emotions, and physical actions. Paul describes it clearly below:

Romans 7:14-18 (ESV)
For we know that the law is spiritual, but I am of the flesh, sold under sin. For I do not understand my own actions. For I do not do what I want, but I do the very thing I hate. Now if I do what I do not want, I agree with the law, that it is good. So now it is no longer I who do it, but sin that dwells within me. **For I know that nothing good dwells in me, that is, in my flesh.** *For I have the desire to do what is right, but not the ability to carry it out.*

Healing Truth No. 10
Temptation is the back door that Satan uses to enter your flesh, so he can lure you into doing things you will really regret afterwards.

The flesh is difficult to master because you live in it 24/7. As an old roommate use to tell me all the time, "Robinson, wherever you go there you are!" You are always with yourself. You are the only person you spend your whole life with. Your flesh goes wherever you go and tries to keep you under its control. God expects the opposite. He expects you to ask the Holy Spirit to control your flesh through your spirit.

Matthew 26:41 (ESV)
Watch and pray that you may not enter into temptation. The spirit indeed is willing, but the flesh is weak.

God wants you to plug in to His Holy Spirit (Power) by surrendering your will to Him moment by moment. When you do this, He charges your spirit taking control of your flesh, stopping it from doing ineffective and bad things. When your spirit is stronger than your flesh, you follow God and receive healing. When your flesh is stronger than your spirit, you are disconnected from the protection you need and tend to do ungodly things that increases pain to you and others.

2 Timothy 1:7 (ESV)
For God gives us a spirit not of fear, but of power and love and <u>self-control</u>.

The Battle between our spirit and our flesh rages until we die. If "self" was a good thing God would not demand that we control it (self-control). He expects us to control it because our flesh is by nature sinful and destructive. We only have victory when our spirits are connected to God's Spirit. Being humans with very "short power cords" we get unplugged often during the day and must plug back in as soon as possible, or our flesh takes control of our lives again. It is a daily *war* we can win only in God's power.

The simplest way of putting it is, "Either you are feeding your spirit or you are feeding your flesh. The one you feed the most will rule your life."

Lesson 1, Prayer Activity 1:   How Much Time Do You Invest in Feeding Your Spirit (Being Plugged into God's Spirit)?

A. How often during the week do you Pray (talk to God)?

Never	Once per week	Once per day	Daily for 30 minutes	Daily for more than 30 minutes

What can you do this week to improve your Prayer time?

B. How often do you read God's Word (the Bible)?

Never	Once per week	Once per day	Daily for 30 minutes	Daily for more than 30 minutes

What can you do this week to improve your Bible reading time?

C. What three sections (books) of the Bible are your favorites to read?

1.
2.
3.

D. What three things inside you keep you from sharing God's Word with others?

1.
2.
3.

Lesson 1, Prayer Activity 2: Activity Instructions

Please mark the areas where you are spiritually struggling on the following tree illustrations.
First, circle the problems that are causing you pain on the Tree of Death (tree of flesh)
illustration. Then, circle where you are weakest on the Tree of Life.

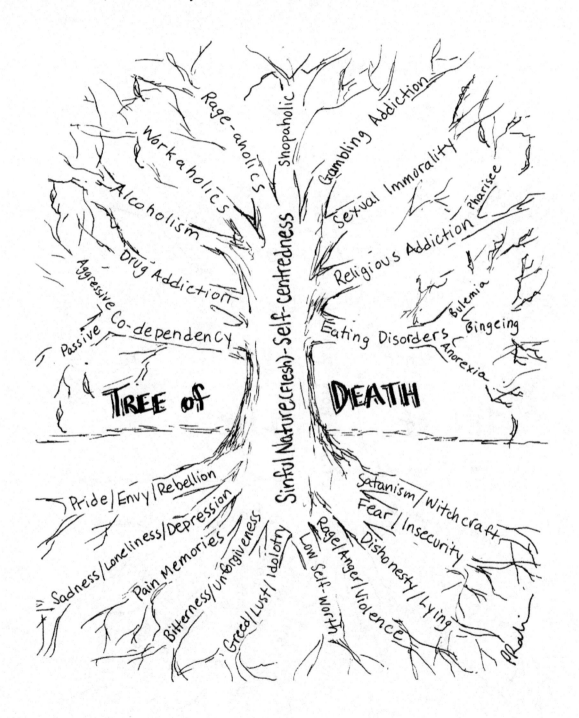

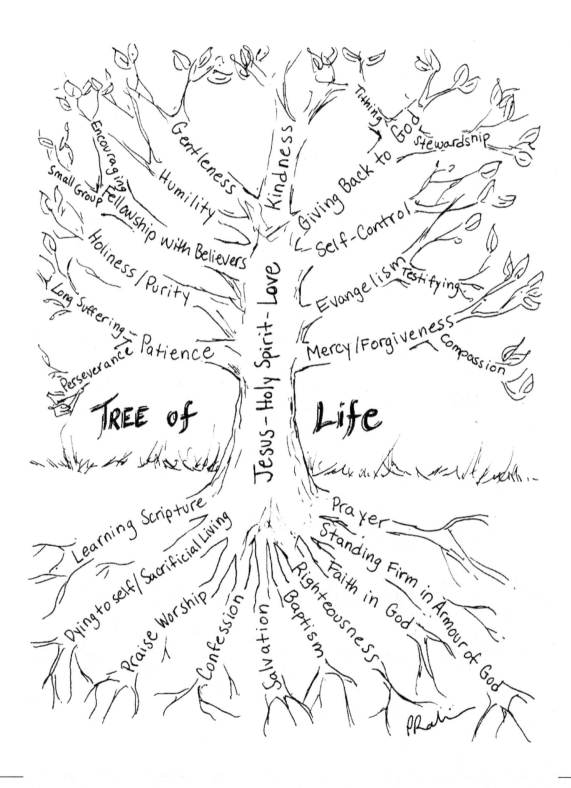

Lesson 1, Prayer Activity 2: Power to Change Your Tree

This information is useful for group sharing (remember each member shares only what they feel comfortable talking about):

A. What are five areas you circled on the Tree of Death sheet?

1.

2.

3.

4.

5.

B. What are five areas you need to improve from the Tree of Life sheet?

1.

2.

3.

4.

5.

C. List below three things out of the ten you listed above that you are willing to let God begin to heal in you this week.

1.

2.

3.

Lesson 1, Prayer Activity 3: Nailing Your Unbelief to the Cross

Nothing changes inside of you until you ask God to change it. When you go to God and ask Him to help you in Jesus' name, He responds because He loves you and because you are His child. You must be willing to name the things in your flesh that are causing you and others pain and let Him take them, believing (faith in Him) that He can and will heal you. God does this because of Jesus' sacrifice on the cross, not because you (we) deserve it. None of us deserves God's mercy. It is a free gift to us paid for with great pain by Jesus.

Some of the main sources of personal pain created by unbelief are:
- Not believing that God exists
- Not believing that God loves you
- Not believing that God can give you power
- Not believing your flesh is your enemy
- Not believing that Jesus died for your sins
- Not believing God will forgive your sins in Jesus' name
- Not believing you have any serious problems
- Not believing God's Word contains your healing
- Not believing the Holy Spirit is real
- Not believing the World is a very dangerous enemy
- Not believing Satan is real and "gunning" for you

Father God, I have struggled with_____for many years, and it is causing me great pain. Please take it from me by washing my spirit clean from it. Increase my faith in You, in the name of Jesus.

After you have prayed and marked the items you want God to remove from inside you, fold your paper and place it in the box at the foot of the cross (if you are in class) or burn it at home without rereading it.

During the next week, thank God every day for taking the burden from you even if your mind tells you it is still there or even if you feel like nothing has happened. This is your flesh trying to stay in control. Praise God ten times morning, noon, and night for your healing.

Deep Healing: Lesson Two

Winning the Battle for the Mind

The Light of Scripture:

> **Romans 13:11-14**
> *And do this, understanding the present time. The hour has come for you to wake up from your slumber, because our salvation is nearer now than when we first believed. The night is nearly over; the day is almost here. So let us put aside the deeds of darkness and put on the armor of light...clothe yourselves with the Lord Jesus Christ, and do not <u>think about how to gratify the desires of the sinful nature.</u>*

A Testimony of God's Deep Healing

I first learned the concepts in the book in a class with Everett. The big eye opener was looking at the tree of death and the tree of life. As I understood the difference between fruit and roots things started to unfold. I soon realized I was lying to myself and others about addictions I had.

As we started to talk about how we cope with pain I realized I had real problems. I started to pray to the Lord to reveal to me patterns that caused me to cycle. This class was good at helping me see that the Lord was holding my hand and that I was not going alone, Jesus was with me. It is so freeing to let the Lord remove the pig poop and start seeing the diamond.

The other big ah ha was the left brain and the right brain and how they operate in our daily lives. I was able to identify who was on my committee in the left side of my brain and I allowed Jesus to remove the ones with critical voices. I also faced the lies that I believed that have controlled me for so many years. I realized that as I forgave the people that have hurt me the Lord was silencing the voices on the committee. I learned that all of my videos that have been recorded from past damaging experiences were still playing in the theater of my mind.

As I plug in daily I'm able to take every thought captive and make it obedient to the Lord; amazingly Jesus is taking away the bad memories. It is incredible to me how the Lord has all the love I needed and never got. It is more than I can hold; I guess that is why now I have so much to give away to my wife and kids.

As painful as it might be, please finish reading this book. Staying where you are at will not make your recovery easier, it will only get worse and hurt more people around you. God bless you.

Joshua S.

Fuzzy Little Treasures

Imagine that you have just gotten home from a week's vacation in Hawaii. As you enter the kitchen, a very strong odor jabs your nose. After recoiling, you move toward your refrigerator and open it very slowly. What you see inside is so disgusting it overwhelms your senses.

All the food that you left in the fridge from Thanksgiving is slightly green and lightly covered in white fuzz. The carcass of what was once the turkey is totally covered in a winter coat. Those left over potatoes are no longer "sweet." Little white pebbles have replaced the petite peas that were once your favorite, and a tub of cheese-like substance sits where the gallon of milk was. The stench comes up like an upper cut taking the top of your head off.
You slam the door shut and run out the back door, gasping for fresh air.

After several minutes recuperating in the back yard, you summon enough courage to head back inside, but first you go into your garage to locate the facemask you used last summer while painting the house. You grab a pair of work gloves and a bucket filled with hot water and degreaser soap, the kind you use for those really "tough" jobs.

Re-entering the kitchen, you clear off the kitchen table and open the fridge door. As quickly as you can, you take all the spoiled food out and place it on the table. When the fridge is empty of all deteriorating nutrition, you start scrubbing the inside of the fridge with hot water and soap. Then you take a dry towel and rub the inside down until it shines.

When you have finished this gruesome task, you step back and notice the main source of the problem, the fridge is unplugged! Plugging it back in you then turn around and grab all of your little fuzzy "treasures" from the table and put them back into the fridge for safekeeping. Satisfied with your hard work, and confident that the fridge is working again, you turn and go upstairs to unpack your suitcase.

What's wrong with this picture?

Many people who need deep healing have gone through various "cleaning" processes only to find that their pain is still there. In this story, the fridge represents your mind. God not only wants to clean it, but He also wants to throw out the garbage and put only good things into it.

God's gift to you is complete inner healing. To do this, He not only removes your rotting "stuff" (negative thoughts, feelings, and desires), but also replaces them with His Holy Spirit. He does this by first helping you get plugged in to His power, a power that never fails. With His power you can stop putting "rotting garbage" (thoughts and images that are hateful, critical, judgmental, fearful, lustful, etc.) back into your mind.

Your flesh is not your friend!

As we learned in Lesson 1, your flesh is not your friend. It impedes your spirit from plugging in to God's Spirit every day. You need to let the Holy Spirit take total control over your flesh, because it is corrupted with the sinful nature. As you plug in, God gives you the spiritual shower you need to become more like Jesus. You actually sabotage yourself when you trust your flesh instead of trusting God. This is not a new concept, God warned long ago about the dangers of our flesh controlling our lives.

> **Jeremiah 17:5**
> *This is what the Lord says: "Cursed is the one who trusts in man, who depends on flesh for his strength and whose heart turns away from the Lord."*

The Battle for the Mind

Winning the battle for your mind becomes a powerful struggle, as your flesh daily wages war against your spirit. All behavior starts in your mind. You make decisions about everything before you actually put those decisions into action. You make hundreds of decisions daily: when to get up, what to wear, when to go to work, what to eat, how fast to drive, etc. Even when you are just sitting still your mind is processing information, and when you are sleeping it speaks to you through dreams and nightmares. In short, the mind never shuts up.

The frightening fact is that your mind also leads you astray from God's healing and toward worldly pain. So how does this happen, and more importantly, how can you stop it?

Healing Truth No. 11
To win the battle for your mind you must control both "super computers" in your brain.

Right Brain and Left Brain Characteristics

It is simply amazing how God created the human mind. All humans have two sides (called hemispheres) to their brains—the left and the right. Each side functions like a "super computer." (You can access some very clear and easy to understand articles about this, just Google the term *left-right brain,* also called *split brain*). You cannot control something if you do not understand what it is; so here is a quick overview of the main differences between the left-side brain (LB) and right-side brain (RB).

1. The LB and RB control different sides of your body.
While it is hard to fathom, God has created the two sides of your brain—each to operate the opposite side of your body. So your LB controls the right side of your body, and the RB controls the left side of the body. This is evident when someone has a stroke (which is very much like a heart attack, but in the brain). If the stroke does not kill, often the patient is crippled on one side of the body. If the left side of the body is handicapped, we know the stroke occurred in the RB. And if the right side is damaged, then it reveals the stroke occurred in the LB.

2. The LB and RB process information very differently.
All day long you are absorbing new information from your environment; this happens through your five senses: smell, taste, sight, hearing, and touch. But as the information comes into your brain, both sides do different things with the same information. The LB breaks it down into categories, identifies it, labels it, and places meaning or value to it. The data is strategically analyzed to see how useful it is for future goals.

For example, you enter a room full of people at a meeting. Your LB immediately breaks down the incoming data as to: how many people are there, what time it is, how long has the meeting been going on, what is the purpose of the meeting, and who you need to connect with to get what you want. In short, the LB takes the whole and breaks it down into parts: processes and strategies.

At the same time, the RB is receiving the same information, but instead of breaking it down it lumps the data all together. It evaluates how the information can help people, how it can improve relationships, how it can impact emotions, and how it can be used for creative action.

So at this same meeting your RB gets excited, because a buzz is going on in the room. People seem upbeat and are talking a lot. There are lots of possibilities to connect with everyone in the room, and there is still plenty of time left to present some creative approaches to the agenda. In short, the RB takes all the parts and creates them into a whole.

3. The LB is more *goal* and *time* driven, while the RB is more *relationship oriented.*
Your LB demands that you use all information to reach goals by certain timelines, regardless of how it impacts people's feelings or needs. It is competitive and wants to "win" (to come out on top) in whatever it is doing. At the same time, the RB demands that you be sensitive to others feelings and ideas, that you be respectful and kind, that you take time to be playful and to enjoy the experience, whatever it happens to be.

4. While the LB is purpose driven, the RB is driven by people and pleasure.
The LB inspires you to be task oriented and value production: what needs to be done now and how much it will cost. The RB is into living life, experiencing it to the fullest, and having fun with others. The LB seeks high quality results and is critical of people and situations. It is less trusting and therefore more controlling. The RB leads you to be overly trusting, to think the best of everyone, and to compromise on quality and achievement if it brings more people together and increases their happiness.

5. Everyone uses both the LB and RB, but not in the same frequency.
God created your mind to be two "super computers" that operate at lightning speeds processing incoming data with staggering complexity. We call this *thinking.* Every individual uses both sides of his or her brain. Most tend to more dominantly use one side of the brain than the other. Yet some people are almost even (50-50) between the two sides of the brain.

Research shows that when comparing males and females (as large gender groups) that men tend to be more LB while women tend to be more RB. Yet it is very important to point out that many men are more dominant RB thinkers and many women are dominant LB thinkers, just as God determined them to be. Every one of us has been created for a purpose which I will discuss later in the book. To help you keep this "split brain" information straight, here is a chart summarizing some major differences between the LB and RB.

Left Brain/Hemisphere	Right Brain/Hemisphere
Controls right side of the body	Controls left side of the body
Center for language/vocabulary	Center for emotions/ feelings; musical, artistic, and athletic talent
Rational, systematic, logical	Impulsive, creative, experiential
Task focused, time driven	People focused, relationship driven
Looks at differences, finds advantages	Looks at similarities, finds common ground
Analytical, sequential thinkers; problem solvers	Holistic thinkers
Competitive, challenge driven	Non-competitive, team driven
Very organizational, hierarchical	Very spontaneous, friendly, playful
Prefers predictability, progress, production	Prefers variety, innovation and invention
Focus is mostly on past and/or future	Focus is mostly on the "now"
Identity – Who you think you are and "should" become	Actor – Who you want to be, wish you were and dream of becoming
Self-Concept – everything you think about self	Self-Esteem – everything you feel about self
Prefers routines, systems that allow for better quality	People, variety, invention are the spices of their lives
Planned, structured developers	Open minded, cross-cultural travelers
Draws on previously accumulated, organized information that often is factual, proven, tested, documented, etc.	Draws on unbounded qualitative patterns that are not organized into sequences, but cluster around images, looks for new solutions to old problems
Logical decision makers: Left brain splits info into categories: distinctions are very important; thinks logically and sequentially; sees cause and effect; problem solving is key focus, and driven toward task completion	Emotional decision makers: Right brain lumps info together; holistic, global thinkers; relationships, associations, connectedness to people highly important, helping, fun, and performing are main focuses

So Left is Right and Right is Left . . . Color me confused!
After going over the left and right brain information several people have said, "Who cares? What does it have to do with my inner healing?"

I always answer the same: "Everything! Even right now your LB and RB are tricking you into thinking none of this information can help you. You need to let God take control of both sides of your brain, if you want to get the healing you need."

God clearly speaks to this split-brain thinking problem creating doubt, which undermines faith, in the following verse:

> **James 1:4**
> *If any of you lack wisdom, he should ask God, who gives generously to all without finding fault, and it will be given to him. But when he asks, he must believe and not doubt, because he who doubts is like a wave of the sea, blown and tossed by the wind. That man should not think he will receive anything from the Lord; he is a double-minded man, unstable in all he does.*

I know that this verse is talking about anyone "having one foot in the world and one foot in God's will for your life". It also is illustrating my point that if both sides of the brain are not totally surrendered to God you will be a "double-minded Christian" and never really experience freedom in Christ. This was a major hurdle in my life, but I assure you that God is more than able to fix your thinking, if you let him.

So how does God go about doing that? A major plan for your mental healing is outlined by the following truths, which are presented in order of importance:

1. You must admit that you do **not** have enough personal power to survive your flesh, the world or Satan. All three are trying to destroy you every day.

2. You were created by God to be spiritually connected to Him, so that you have the power to fulfill the purpose He created you for. He gave you "will power" (choice) to choose, if you want to have a personal connection with Him or not. Trading your will for His is the beginning of your healing journey.

3. You must accept Jesus (His son) as your Lord (Master) to be fully connected to God.

4. You can only connect to God in Jesus name (there is no name under Heaven by which you can be saved. Only He died for your sins).

5. When connected to God you then receive His Power (the Holy Spirit, which is God Himself) which is greater than your flesh, the world or Satan.

6. Your flesh cannot be controlled by you (self-control) without God's Holy Spirit living in you. Only God's power is strong enough to protect you.

7. You can only win the war with your flesh, when you have won the war within your mind (on both sides of your brain). This war rages until the day you die.

8. God reprograms (refurbishes) your mind only when you are connected to Him by His Holy Spirit.

9. This mental refurbishing is called Deep Healing (Deep Cleaning). God is actually resetting your thinking to be what it needs to be to fulfill the purpose for which He created you.

10. Your real purpose in life now becomes helping others take their Journey into God's Deep Healing.

Everything in your mind is directly related to learning through your five senses: **seeing, hearing, touching, smelling, and tasting**. Even before birth your mind was recording information from the outside world. Like all computers it stockpiles data into files that you access for daily decision-making (LB). It also creates extensive picture albums of everything you see and experience while growing up (RB). These two systems of retaining information are call "memories."

Healing Truth No. 12
The garbage you allow into your brain will negatively influence all of your life decisions and can keep you separated (disconnected) from God.

We want to think the "world" is a paradise that has no problems, when in fact it is a very fractured home we live on. As I sit in the hot sun on my back porch sipping cold ice tea, I tend to reject that view of Earth and Humanity. Yet the sun rays and my ice tea do nothing to stop the many wars, diseases, famines, corruption, abuse, dishonesty, earthquakes, and hurricanes destroying families every day. To add to the negativity, television shows, super mega movies, newspapers, and internet pornography infect many people with fears, insecurities, anger, and lust; all of which is mental "corruption" or "garbage." Much of this garbage comes in without you even knowing it has entered your mind.

I call this corruption "mind pollution". It acts just like a "Trojan worm" that is infecting the operating system of your computer. It requires a power greater than you to "wipe your hard drive (brain) clean."

About a year ago, I opened an email from someone I did not know. The message said it was urgent, so I clicked on it without thinking. Instantly my computer went nuts. My security program started sending me messages that a Trojan worm had invaded my computer and was taking over. I freaked out until I remembered what my good friend Ron told me, "Do not turn your computer off. If you think you have a virus, call me first."

I called Ron and he had me check my virus program to see if the invader had been quarantined, which it had. He then told me it was OK to turn off the computer and bring it to him.

When I took my computer to him, I figured it would only take a few minutes for him to kick the worm out, and I would be on my way. After examining it, he told me he would need to keep it for a couple of days, so he could wipe the hard drive clean.

I was very upset at first. I thought that wiping my hard drive clean would destroy my valuable files, documents, and programs.

Ron just laughed and told me to leave it to the "Master." I had to trust him to do what he said he would do, and Ron returned the computer in its proper working order, without losing any of my files!

Healing Truth No. 13
To have your "super computers" refurbished, you must give them back to their Creator.

When you have viruses in the computers in your brain, you need to go to the Master for help. Removing these "Trojan worms" from your thinking requires expert skill, as they are totally different viruses. Praise God that He is the Creator and knows exactly how to wipe your "hard drive" (brain) clean without losing any of your important memories. Praise God that He can and will renew your mind by removing the lies that for years kept you from praying to Him. The lies that keep you unplugged from His power.

> **1 Peter 4:7**
> *The end of all things is near. Therefore be **clear-minded** and **self-controlled** so that you can pray.*

How Your Left-Side Brain Works Against You

The most damaging force within the left side of the brain is your "inner voice" or "self-talk." It is located where your vocabulary (word) center is located. It influences you by "talking" to you within your thinking. In short, it is the personal conversation you have with yourself all day long. The inner voice is a good influence, if it has been programmed with positive (godly) information and truths. It is a bad influence, if it has been programmed with negative (worldly) lies.

The negative inner voice has many characteristics that identify it: lying to self and others, fear, worry, critical thoughts of self and others, jealous thoughts, pride, and selfishness. All self-devaluations have only one true purpose—to destroy your life and others lives. It is often referred to as "stinking thinking" in recovery programs.

As your inner voice is trained by others and the world to become negative, it takes on self-destructive techniques. In short, instead of being your best friend it becomes your worst enemy. Please consider the following identifying characteristics of a negative inner voice.

Negative Inner Voice Characteristics

1. It is judgmental; highly critical of you and others.
2. It is jealous, unforgiving, and vengeful.
3. It hurts others while telling you it's for their own good.
4. It is manipulative and deceitful.
5. It lies to you to deceive and control you.
6. It isolates you from positive people and from God so it can control you.
7. It sets you up to fail repeatedly by choosing toxic relationships.
8. It is fearful, worries excessively, and tells you there is no hope for you.
9. It is controlling of you and others.
10. It is verbally abusive toward you, it is your worst bully.

Healing Truth No. 14
Just because you think it, doesn't make it true.

Perfectionists are really Worry Worshippers

Many people worry, worry, and worry about everything. Your negative inner voice hounds you day and night, telling one lie after another, and you believe every one of them. Some of its biggest lies are:

- You have to be more than you are.
- You have to be better looking than you are.
- You have to be smarter than you are.
- You have to be holier than you are.
- You have to be kinder than you are.
- You have to be more fun than you are.
- You have to be "perfect" to be successful.

This type of negative thinking causes much stress and leads to repeated failures in relationships, as well as causing major health issues. It never stops talking to you telling you that you can never be satisfied, because you will always fall short of being "perfect". You will never be happy because you are so imperfect, and your mind keeps piling it on no matter how good of a job you do.

In short, listening and agreeing with your negative inner voice will destroy everything you hope to have in life, because negative thinking leads to negative behavior.

> "Watch your thoughts, they become words
> Watch your words, they become actions
> Watch your actions they become habits
> Watch your habits they become character
> Watch your character it will become your destiny."
> By Frank Outlaw (poster sold at www.jaguared.com)

Your "Negative Inner Voice" Is Nothing But A Big Bad Bully

When I started trusting Jesus, I stopped taking garbage into my body. Then my mind started to work the way it was created to work. As I praised God more and read His Word daily, I suddenly realized just what my negative inner voice really was—a bully!

Bullies rule with fear and intimidation, but *by plugging in to God's power you will receive the spiritual power to stand firm against all of your bully's threats.* In fact, it is a persecutor of your soul. And within your mind (the main computer running your flesh), your left brain and right brain are full of viruses that need to be removed. The main virus in the left side of your brain is your negative inner voice. Praise God, removing mental pollution is His specialty!

Take a brain bath; let God wash away your negative inner voice every day!

> **Romans 12:2**
> *Do not conform any longer to the pattern of this world, but be transformed by the renewing of your mind. Then you will be able to test and approve what God's will is—his good, pleasing and perfect will.*

To find complete healing, you must examine how your mind keeps leading you back into self-destructive behavior patterns over and over and over again. The usual answer is, "your negative inner voice." It has been programmed to destroy you from an early age, and with God's power you can reprogram it before it is too late.

What goes on in your head strongly influences your decision making, which directs your behavior choices. This, in turn, decides your success in life. Let's take a closer look at how to turn your negative thoughts into positive ones.

1. Read and memorize scripture daily. God's Word will wash your mind clean.

2. List what your inner voice is telling you. Seeing it on paper helps you see how negative it is, and then you can change it by rewriting it.

3. Tape record you talking. The negative inner voice speaks through your mouth all the time. Decide if what you hear coming out of your mouth honors God and those you love. When it doesn't, change it.

4. Identify who is on your committee. These are the most significant people who first programed (good and bad) your operating system (Inner Voice). Figure out where the negative thoughts first started; what person, or what event led to you thinking each thought. Replace negative thoughts with positive ones. Replace negative devaluations with scripture verses to help restore your mind to God's will.

5. Learn to discern between God's voice and your committee members voices. Identify who is really talking to you? Is the message helping or hurting you and others?

6. Your negative inner voice can also be controlled by Satan. Satan enters through what others say and the media: pictures, books, movies, TV shows, music, newspapers, lectures, etc. Temptations are projected into our thoughts every day through these sources. Limit things that put negativity into your mind faster than you can learn scripture. For instance, when I stopped listening to rock and roll my negative thoughts and behavior decreased noticeably.

7. Stop hanging around people who tell you negative things about yourself and others. Spend time with those who are positive in their outlook on life and who praise God rather than curse men.

8. Get help with your negative inner voice. It will always tell you that you can do it alone, which is how it wins over you. You must always work with people who have more spiritual maturity than you do. They will help you with your "stinking thinking."

9. Read Christian articles and books that will help you control your thinking. You will find many of them under the title of "self-talk."

10. Praise God by thanking Him for everything you have. By doing this daily you will be plugging into the Power you need to clean your hard drive. You also will be able to better identify the negative thoughts that have been hiding inside your thinking for years.

Healing Truth No. 15
God does not negotiate with terrorists, and your negative inner voice terrorizes you every day. It is holding you for a ransom that will never be paid.

When you start to let God change your negative inner voice it will freak out, rebel and fight to keep control over you. It will kick, bite and threaten you for surrendering your will to God instead of trusting in it.

Do not be worried. Worrying is just your negative inner voice trying to keep you locked in fear. Don't panic. Just trust God more than you trust your own mind. One of my favorite quotes from St. Augustine provides a solution:

> "Do not try to understand so that you may believe,
> but believe that you might understand."

Your inner voice often says, "Wait a minute. What if . . .?"

One of your negative inner voices tactics is to always question and doubt God's ability to help you. By undermining your thinking it continues to hold valuable territory within your mind and therefore, it can still negatively influence how you to think, feel and experience pain. It uses you to block God from giving you the help you need to take control over it and the other self- destructive parts of your mind.

Get mad! Attack the negativity in your mind! It is not who you were created to be! Self-hatred statements in your inner voice do not come from God. They are poisonous to you and to all of your relationships. Fight back by plugging in to God's Spirit to get spiritual power to override the lies in your head. Let God teach you to love yourself by reading God's Word and memorizing scripture to replace the world's lies with God's truth.

> Either you let God
> change and control
> your inner voice for good
> or your inner voice will
> control and change you for bad!

Lesson 2, Prayer Activity 1: Stopping the Negative Inner Voice

Rate the following **Negative Inner Voice Characteristics in your mind.**
Not there = NT   Sometimes There = ST   Always There = AT

1. ___It is judgmental; highly critical of you and others.
2. ___It is jealous, unforgiving, and vengeful.
3. ___It hurts others while saying it's for their own good.
4. ___It is manipulative and deceitful.
5. ___It lies.
6. ___It isolates you from positive people and from God, so it can control you.
7. ___It sets you up to fail repeatedly by choosing toxic relationships.
8. ___It is fearful, worries excessively and tells you there is no hope for you.
9. ___It is controlling of you and others.
10. ___It is verbally abusive toward you.

Now take five minutes to quickly write answers to these questions:

A. What are some of the most powerful negative words your mind tells you?

B. How do you spiritually "stand firm" when Satan attacks your inner voice with lies and other negative thoughts?

C. What can you do to take the offensive in the spiritual fight within your mind?

Lesson 2, Prayer Activity 2: Who's On Your Committee?

Take five minutes to write your five most significant committee members (mental programmers) and list how they, through your negative inner voice, still influence your decision-making and behavior today.

Identify one negative thought each committee member planted into your mind, and discuss how it still affects you today.

Example: Father yelling at you as a kid for the hundredth time: "How many times do I have to tell you that's not how to do it. What are you stupid? You're more trouble than you are worth!"

<u>Committee Members</u>   <u>Negative Thoughts/Behaviors from them</u>

1.

2.

3.

4.

5.

Lesson 2, Prayer Activity 3: The Truth Will Set You Free

In the spaces numbered below, write out five negative statements (lies) that your inner voice (self-talk) tells you about yourself. Then go back and write one of God's truths for each lie you wrote down.

Inner voice lies: example = I can never be forgiven for what I have done, it's too bad and too late to be forgiven.

God's truth: example = Jesus says in Luke 17:3-4

> *"So watch yourselves. "If your brother sins, rebuke him, and if he repents, forgive him. If he sins against you seven times in a day, and seven times comes back to you and says, 'I repent,' forgive him.*

1. Lie Number One =

God's truth is =

2. Lie Number Two =

God's truth is =

3. Lie Number Three =

God's truth is =

4. Lie Number Four =

God's truth is =

5. Lie Number Five =

God's truth is =

Lesson 2, Prayer Activity 4: Separating Left from Right

As you read the list of personality characteristics, check the eight (only eight) that best describe you. Place your checkmarks under the side of the brain you think it belongs on.

Personality Characteristics	Right Brain	Left Brain
I am task focused, time driven		
I am spontaneous, friendly, and playful		
I prefer planned, structured activities		
I have natural musical, artistic, athletic abilities		
I tend to be emotional, passionate, and sensitive		
I tend to be competitive, challenge driven		
I focus mostly on the past and/or the future		
I am attracted to people, variety, invention		
I look for similarities, common ground with others		
I am an organizational, hierarchical thinker		
I focus mostly on "now" (the present, today)		
I like following routines and systems that achieve quality		
I am open minded, accepting of different people		
I am a logical decision maker who likes facts		
I quickly notice situational differences, advantages		
I am non-competitive, team driven, and like cooperation		
I prefer increasing production, obtaining results, and pursuing goals		
I am an analytical, a sequential problem solver		
I prefer variety, innovation, and creativity		
I am an emotional decision maker; often I am impulsive		
I am very people focused, relationship driven		

Lesson 2, Prayer Activity 5: Nailing Your Negative Inner Voice to the Cross

Nothing changes inside of you until you ask God to change it. When you go to God and ask Him to help you in Jesus' name, He responds because He loves you and because you are His child. You must be willing to name the things in your flesh that are causing you and others pain and let Him take them, believing (faith in Him) that He can and will heal you. God does this because of Jesus' sacrifice on the cross, not because you (we) deserve it. None of us deserves God's mercy. It is a free gift to us paid for with great pain by Jesus.

Some of the main sources of mental and relationship pain are:
- Lies within your thinking
- Critical, judgmental thoughts toward others
- Critical, judgmental thoughts toward yourself
- Jealous thoughts
- Vengeful thoughts
- Racist and/or sexist thoughts
- Lustful, sexually immoral thoughts
- Isolating thoughts that keep you separated from God and others

Father God, I have struggled with_____for many years, and it is causing me great pain. Please take it from me by washing my spirit clean from it. Increase my faith in you Father, in the name of Jesus.

After you have prayed and marked the items you want God to remove from inside you, please fold your paper and place it in the box at the foot of the cross (if at home burn this page without rereading it).

During the next week thank God every day for taking it, even if your mind tells you it is still there. If you feel nothing has happened, this is your flesh trying to stay in control. Praise God ten times morning, noon, and night for your healing.

Deep Healing: Lesson Three

If Your Left One Doesn't Get Ya, Your Right One Will!

The Light of Scripture:

Proverbs 14:12
There is a way that <u>seems</u> right to a man, but in the end it leads to death.

A Testimony of God's Deep Healing

My name is Dave and I am in my mid-fifties, married with grown children. All my life I have been listening to a voice in my head that has brought me nothing but fear and worry. I have been always questioning everything, such as: "Where is God?", "Is this as good as it gets?", and "Why am I here?"

I felt so alone that even though I knew 100's of people I always felt isolated, unable to connect to people and to God. I had major anger problems and had hurt many of my family members deeply.

Then I took the class and learned how to "plug-in" to God. Every day I surrender my life to Jesus and God pours his love into me. My negative inner voice is no longer controlling my life and now I can understand God's Word. I actually have gotten past the self-hatred and know that God has created me for a purpose.

Through this amazing information I am now taking a journey that I only thought happened to others, never to me. God's plan is so much better than the one I have been listening to. I have learned to let God's Holy Spirit transform my mind and heart.

I know you can find the same inner peace if you let God take control of your life.

Dave Z.

This Is Weird, But Interesting!

fi yuo cna raed tihs, yuo hvae a sgtrane mnid too. Cna
yuo raed tihs? Olny 55 plepoe out of 100 can.
I cdnuolt blveiee taht I cluod aulaclty uesdnatnrd waht I was rdanieg. The
phaonmneal pweor of the hmuan mnid, aoccdrnig to rscheearch at
Cmabrigde Uinervtisy—it dseno't mtaetr in waht oerdr the ltteres in a word are,
the olny iproamtnt tihng is taht the frsit and lsat ltteer be in the rghit pclae. The
rset can be a taotl mses and you can sitll raed it whotuit a pboerlm.
 Tihs is bcuseae the huamn mnid deos not raed ervey lteter by istlef, but the wrod as a
 wlohe. Azanmig, huh? And I awlyas tghuhot slpeling was ipmorantt!

Left-Side Translation of the above statements:

If you can read this, you have a strange mind too. Can you read this? Only 55 people out of 100 can. I couldn't believe that I could actually understand what I was reading. The phenomenal power of the human mind, according to research at Cambridge University—it doesn't matter in what order the letters in a word are, the only important thing is that the first and last letter be in the right place. The rest can be a total mess and you can still read it without a problem. This is because the human mind does not read every letter by itself, but the word as a whole. Amazing huh? And I always thought spelling was important!

The words above seem scrambled and so mixed up that they make no sense, but the message is actually quite easy to read if you do so with the right side of your brain rather than your left side.

Remember that your vocabulary center is on the left side of your brain. The left side identifies every letter and assesses the order they are in to match the sequence with a word in its memory banks that has that exact spelling. But the right side of your brain (only once a word has been learned correctly by your left side) can recognize the scrambled word by its "picture" located in your memory.

To control your behavior you must be able to control both sides of your brain.

Romans 8: 5-6 (ESV)
For those who live according to the flesh set their minds on the things of the flesh, but those who live according to the Spirit set their minds on the things of the Spirit. For to set the mind on the flesh is death, but to set the mind on the Spirit is life and peace.

So how can you take charge of your right-side brain?
1. You must first understand how the Right Side works.
2. You then must identify what "bad" movies are playing in your mind.
3. You then need to pray and ask God to remove these movies from your memories.
4. You finally allow God to put positive, godly movies into your mind.

Summary of Right-Side Brain (RB) Key Points

Along with your left-side brain, the right side of your brain is another wonderful super computer that God has programmed to do some amazing things. For example:

- All your emotions exist in the right side of your brain. All feelings originate from there.
- RB dominant people tend to be "experiential" (learn by doing) learners.
- Your mental pictures, images, and imagination come from this side.
- RB dominant people tend to be more relationship oriented: compassionate and merciful.
- RB dominant people see animals as friends and family members rather than as "just pets."
- The right side of the brain hosts all your creativity and "thinking out of the box."
- RB dominant people tend to be artistic, love dancing, painting, sewing, etc.
- RB dominant people tend to be athletic and love playing sports.
- RB dominant people tend to be musical and love playing instruments and singing.
- RB dominant people tend to smile more, laugh louder, and touch more.
- RB dominant people tend to love cooperation, teamwork, win-win thinking; they are less competitive than LB dominant people.
- RB dominant people tend to prefer variety in everything, especially people, so they prefer friends that are "different" from themselves.
- RB people tend to be more impulsive and often have difficulties with self-discipline and critical comments made about them.

Understanding how the right side of your brain influences your life choices is just as important as comprehending how the left side of your brain impacts your decision making. On the right side there are very powerful characteristics that either are working with you to find healing, or are working against you to cause pain.

Stocking Your Mind with "New Movies"

You have a "Theater of the Mind" in the right side of your brain. In it, you are the director and producer of whatever images are "playing." You mix and match memories from your past with other images you have put in your "video vault." All of your experiences provide your "production company" with new material. Watching TV shows, playing video games, looking at pornography, and reading romantic novels and gossip magazines can greatly increase the number of corrupt images in your mind. As mentioned in the previous lesson, "garbage in means garbage out."

Many "dreams" are retaliation movies against someone who hurt you or wronged you in some way. In these fantasies, you are telling them exactly what you think and how you feel. You are doing things to them that you would never do in reality, but in fantasy it sure feels good to get even with them! Other fantasies may focus on making millions of dollars, paying off all your debts and still having lots of money left for traveling, buying things, and helping the poor.

Often your mental theater plays horror movies that keep your fear level high. Images that scare you to death are presented, and very evil things are happening to you. Sometimes these images come from actual horror movies or events you have read about. At other times, they are created by horrific things that have happened during your life.

The mind uses these images to frighten, threaten and control you with fear. Like the negative inner voice, you also have a negative movie director who uses the mental images to punish you so it can control your behavior.

Healing Truth No. 16
You are responsible for everything that plays in your theater.

Daydreaming

As you have learned, the right side of the brain operates with pictures, sounds, colors, dreams, images, and voids (blank spaces in our thinking). Daydreaming manipulates you with "movies" of what could have been and what should be. It often replays past events with different outcomes, producing fantasies to replace the many realities you hate facing every day.

For instance, when you find reality "boring" you will often take a mental trip up into your theater to watch something more uplifting, more enlightening and more stimulating. In these mental vacations you always win, always fall in love, always get the promotion and always get justice for past wrongs.

Unfortunately, when you return to reality you realize that nothing has really changed. Life is still "boring" and disappointing compared to your fantasies. In fact, reality is even more unappealing; because of the success you just had in your fantasy.

The most destructive part of these types of "mental vacations" is that they require you to leave the "now." So even while your body is sitting in reality (school, work, home, church, etc.), your mind is a million miles away. At these times you are not concentrating on what is happening around you in the present, you are lost in your gray matter which leaves you in a very vulnerable place. This often happens when talking on the phone or tweeting. People die everyday in a split second when go on "vacation" in their minds on the highways, at work and even at home.

I already stated how the negative inner voice can cause a traffic accident if you listen to it instead of paying attention to driving safely. The same thing happens while you are driving with the right side of your brain. Only this time you don't hear anything. You just see pictures of yourself being somewhere other than in your car. When this occurs, your concentration is not on operating the vehicle as much as it is on what you are "imagining," leaving you and others at great risk. We sometimes call this "spacing out."

One of the things I stress when working with individuals is that they be "grounded," which is the skill of "living in the now." I help them learn how to stay focused on now, whether it is good or bad, so they can stay in control of their minds. If you cannot control your mind, you will never be able to control your behavior. If you cannot stay focused on now, you will be misled into making bad decisions by the pollution stored in your brain.

Healing Truth No. 17
Isolating from others by withdrawing into fantasy will keep you mentally sick, emotionally crazy, and ineffective in your relationships.

One of the most self-destructive parts of mentally leaving reality is that you can't stay on your mental vacations for long unless you use something to prolong the "trip." When people are unhappy, they love to *medicate*. This is a recovery term that means people put things into their bodies that make their minds go into dream mode and stay there longer.

For example: alcohol, coffee, drugs, viewing porn, sexual acts, gambling, compulsive shopping, smoking, eating sweets and many more sources stimulate the release of a natural drug called *dopamine* in our brains. Dopamine leaves us with the feeling of elation or a "emotional high" thus offsetting the drudgery of living in reality. Addictions are driven by such physical and emotional highs.

When you use these escape patterns repeatedly, they stop being just self-reinforcing negative compulsions, but become harmful habits called addictions. At this point your bad habits are controlling you rather than you controlling them, which simply means you are "out-of - control". God's healing puts you "in-control" of your mind and behavior.

When your mind becomes controlled by negativity and world pollution, your reality becomes a "living nightmare." Health, wealth, and relationships can all come crashing down, leaving you worse off than when you first started living in your "head"; or should we say, living on Fantasy Island.

Healing Truth No. 18
You are either downloading pollution from the world or holiness from God, who is the real internet, because He is Reality.

So why does watching mental movies make you feel so right, feel so good?

Giving up mental movies is never easy as you are very attached to your private collections. Over the years these bad toys have become your most prized processions. While others have let you down in real life your fantasies remain loyal. They keep on giving you everything you want to see and hear. They make you feel good even when you are being bad.

Fantasies are designed to replace your negative feelings. So it only makes sense that those negative feelings also act like triggers that send you into medicating behavior patterns within your mind. "Acting in" patterns first and then dysfunctional "acting out" behavior second.

There was a saying during the '60s, "If it feels good do it!" Letting your feelings make your decisions is letting your feelings control your behavior. Sooner or later you want your fantasy life to become reality. For example, fantasizing often leads to secret lives. You spend time every week thinking and doing things you don't want others to know about: affairs, stealing, porn, gambling, excessive binging with food, alcohol, drugs and gossiping are all examples of this.

Having a "secret life" gives people a false sense of power and freedom. This acting out often matches the mental fantasies they are having with their mental images and, in turn, adds to their video vault collection. Secret lives are very rewarding until the secret is uncovered— then the price you and others have to pay is very high and very painful.

Somebody Owes Me Something!

One major emotional trigger is the feeling of *entitlement*. This feeling has been around long before this current generation got labeled with it. It lives in the right side of the brain and does not care about facts, such as God's and civil laws. Many people believe they have the right to do whatever they imagine or dream. Many seek money, objects, improper relationships, and thrill-seeking experiences they often cannot afford (such as racing four- wheel drive trucks up muddy hills or going on dream vacations). Cars, boats, electronic equipment, bigger TVs, shopping to get more clothes, gambling, and eating in high end restaurants are some examples of this entitlement life style.

Often, these entitlement demands are really attempts to fill in a deep emptiness people feel inside; an emptiness that comes from injustice (painful abuse) that happened to them during their early years. They believe someone "owes" them for the pain they had to suffer while growing up. It grows a root of bitterness which leads to trash talking and lying.

> **Romans 3:13-14**
> *Their throats are open graves; their tongues practice deceit.*
> *The poison of vipers is on their lips.*
> *Their mouths are full of cursing and bitterness.*

A familiar saying women often say about men acting badly is, "They are just little boys playing with their toys." Unfortunately, women also have many dreams, desires, and habits that are just as self-destructive. Knowing this many people still refuse to give up their mental toys because these toys have become their "best friends." Perhaps these mental friends have been with you since early childhood, when you first suffered pain and loss in relationships. In dysfunctional families, our minds are often the only place where we had any sense of being in control. The only place we felt safe, normal, and happy; even if it was just a fantasy we came out the "winner".

To those in deep pain, giving up such mental friends would be like giving up their right arm. In reality, refusing to give up this sense of entitlement will determine your worldly destiny and eternal future in a very negative way.

Since most people suffering in pain have few friends, they often share their painful thoughts and feelings with their mental images to fill in for their loss of intimacy. The Theater of the Mind is like a friend's house where you can always go for comfort.

This is especially attractive after a hard day of trying to make it in reality. The more you go to this theater, the more you become a prisoner of fantasy and the less you are able to function successfully in reality. But to receive healing, you must first be willing to leave this "old friend" who is now your worst enemy, and give up your "mind toys."

The good news is that Jesus will be the friend and family you never had, *if* you surrender the battle you are having with your flesh to Him. He will remove the friends in your mind that really are your worst threats to being healed. He will take the pain away in reality, so you do not need to escape into fantasy.

Healing Truth No. 19
When it gets too tough to stand before men, kneel before God. You'll stumble and fall less when you are on your knees.

Whatever the images are, if they do not honor God, you must let Him wash your mind clean of them. Asking God to remove them from your brain and to replace them with thoughts that are affirming to Him and to you is a superb way to take back your mind. Freedom from this mental prison only comes when you ask God to wash your mind clean of memories, emotions, and fantasies that dishonor Him. When you surrender your will to Him, God will lead you away from the unwholesome thinking that leads you into sinful actions. As blessed by God as King David was, he too sinned in a major way and brought pain into his life. He was healed when he cried out to God.

> **Psalm 51:2**
> *Wash away all my iniquity and cleanse me from my sin.*

Healing Truth No. 20
God is real, no matter how you feel. Nothing changes inside you until you let God change it.

People, being proud and spiritually stubborn, tend to drag their feet in giving over to God the very things that are killing them. They hang on to the lie that says they can do it themselves with a "little help" from God. Another year goes by and they are back exactly where they were originally: still hurting themselves, and still hurting others as they continue to live in their fantasies. Then they often blame God for their choices and failures (negative inner voice) instead of taking responsibility and ownership for their own choices.

> **Colossians 1:21**
> *Once you were alienated from God and were enemies in your minds because of your evil behavior.*

You cannot solve your problem because *you* are the problem. Your flesh tries to negotiate the terms of surrender with God, but God does not bargain with kidnappers. The great news is that once you have completely surrendered, God is more than willing and able to put your personality and life back together the way it was supposed to be before you surrendered your mind and life to fantasy!

Either God controls your life or your flesh controls it. Thinking that you can be in control without God's power (plugging in) is insanity.

Lesson 3, Prayer Activity 1: Inventorying the Video Vault in Your Mind

Please pray and ask God to tell you how to answer the following questions: List

four fantasies (mental movies) that you frequently replay in your mind?

    1.
    2.
    3.
    4.

What four emotions trigger you to fantasize (enter the theater in your mind)?

    1.
    2.
    3.
    4.

What are four traumatic memories that haunt you (mentally replay over and over in your thoughts and dreams)?

    1.
    2.
    3.
    4.

What are four memories (mental toys) you don't want to give up to God?

    1.
    2.
    3.
    4.

Lesson 3, Prayer Activity 2: Assessing Sources of Mental Pollution

Rate each source by marking how much time you spend using each one to gain impure thoughts, words, and images for your "mental movies."

Sources for Mental pollution	No problem, I use them very little	A struggle, it is hard to put them down	They own me, I am addicted to them
Magazines			
Books			
Television Shows			
Movies, DVDs			
Internet			
Video Games			
Laptop, Notebook, Tablet			
Cellphone			
Smartphone			
Car Radio			
Social Media: Facebook, Twitter, etc.			
"Friends" who constantly lead you into sin and painful situations			

Lesson 3, Prayer Activity 3: Nailing Your Video Vault to the Cross

Nothing changes inside of you until you ask God to change it. When you go to God and ask Him to help you in Jesus' name, He responds because He loves you and because you are His child. You must be willing to name the things in your flesh that are causing you and others pain and let Him take them, believing (faith in Him) that He can and will heal you. God does this because of Jesus' sacrifice on the cross, not because you (we) deserve it. None of us deserves God's mercy. It is a free gift to us paid for with great pain by Jesus.

Some of the main sources of mental and relationship pain from the right side of your brain (Theater of your Mind) are:

- Memories of traumatic events you have experienced.
- Mental videos that keep replaying your acts of sin from the past.
- Images from movies, magazines, and the internet that should not be in your mind, but you keep looking at them while fantasizing.
- Fantasies that tempt your desires until you do sinful things.
- Not functioning effectively in reality because you are spending so much time in fantasy.
- Dreams that show you being anyone other than who you are.
- Anger and rage about your life.
- Anger and rage mental videos about your life.

Father God, I have struggled with_____for many years, and it is causing me great pain. Please take it from me by washing my spirit clean from it. Please increase my faith in you Father, in the name of Jesus.

During the next week thank God every day for washing your mind clean, even if your mind tells you nothing has changed, or you feel like your prayer was not answered. Praise God ten times morning, noon, and night for your healing. By your Faith you will be healed. If you need more faith ask God for more faith.

Deep Healing: Section Two
Winning the War Within

The Light of Scripture:

Ephesians 2:1-6

As for you, you were dead in your transgressions and sins, in which you used to live when you followed the ways of this world and of the ruler of the kingdom of the air, the spirit who is now at work in those who are disobedient.

All of us also lived among them at one time, gratifying the cravings of our sinful nature and following its desires and thoughts. Like the rest, we were by nature objects of wrath.

But because of his great love for us, God, who is rich in mercy, made us alive with Crist even when we were dead in transgressions—it is by grace you have been saved, through faith—and this not from yourselves, it is the gift of God-not by works, so that no one can boast.

For we are God's workmanship, <u>created in Christ Jesus to do good works, which God prepared in advance for us to do</u>.

A Testimony to God's Deep Healing

(email) Getting to work on the lesson for tonight before bed…looking forward to it honestly, so thank you for that. Homework I am actually eager to do because I know every time I do I grow and improve into the kind of "me" I've been desperately seeking but unable to obtain. ☺

Here's what my answer is to your question, "What are three things you learned in this book (class) that you are grateful to God for? Everett - Honest in failure, faithful to God, Broken but unafraid.

I will miss you both immensely. Your class has matured me in SO many ways I had been seeking to grow but hadn't the slightest idea what I could do to stop stunting my growth. I can't thank you enough.

Jackie S.

Deep Healing: Lesson Four

Understanding the Heart of the Problem

The Light of Scripture:

Psalm 53:1
The fool says in his heart, "There is no God."

A Testimony to God's Deep Healing

Making the decision to drive 45 minutes one evening a week for 14 weeks was the easy part of committing to the Deep Healing course! That I needed it was not a question. God used it to change my life in a way I never thought possible. That this would be a commitment for life was the question I had to determine.

While I clearly knew that God had undeservedly blessed me in many ways, my biggest challenge was my NIV (negative inner voice), which would always question things and imply negative motives to so many events . . . and so many people!

Many concepts of the course made a huge impact in my life, but the simple and effective concept of PG10X has been huge! "Praising God ten times" or for ten things, or for ten people, or for ten blessings . . . Every time a negative thought tries to dominate my thinking, it just squeezes out the Evil One and keeps me plugged in and connected to Jesus, His purpose for me, and His continued direction for my day and for my life.

God has allowed me free choices, and I choose to live for Him. I look forward to more time with Him until I can forever be with Him!

Praise be to Jesus!

Thank you Everett and Denise for being the tools God used, and for the wisdom God gives you!

Menno F.

5:55 in the Morning

In 1990 I went into recovery for my self-destructive behavior (addiction). In the early days of my recovery nothing seemed to get better because I wasn't trusting God to heal me. I thought I had to do everything myself. Instead of finding inner peace I found that things just got worse. I was depressed and had given up hope that God would ever heal me. Then, due to my continued failings, self-hatred and constant negativity Denise had enough and left me. Now I was alone except for our two little dogs, Sweetie and Arlo. I stopped praying and went into a deep mental hole. Nothing seemed important anymore and I figured I would never be happy again, let alone make it to heaven.

God often calls (speaks to) us when we are going through what the bible calls a desert experience. It is during these heavy trials and times of grieving that we are more open to listening to Him instead of telling Him how things are going to be.

One night as I was laying on the floor, crying and feeling sorry for the many people I had hurt, Arlo and Sweetie began licking my face. Usually I would have just push them away, but I didn't have the energy to. Then God spoke to me through His Spirit. He simply said "Psalm 51".

I had not read my bible for weeks and I was pretty sure that I had never read Psalm 51 as I believed the Psalms were of little use for "current" day problems. Boy, was I ever wrong!

As I started reading this Psalm, God spoke to my spirit in such a powerful way that I began my healing process at that very moment. Every word was alive with meaning and power. I felt loved by God as I had never felt loved before. I felt God's shadow pass over me bringing me inner peace and hope. Hope that I was not only wanted by Him but that I was also valued as His child. While I had felt God's love before in brief moments during my life this time I was empowered with it by the Holy Spirit. And those verses became the foundation for everything I have written or taught since then.

Psalm 51:10-13
Create in me a pure heart, O God, and renew a steadfast spirit within me. Do not cast me from your presence or take your Holy Spirit from me, Restore to me the joy of your salvation and grant me a willing spirit, to sustain me. Then I will teach transgressors your ways, and sinners will turn back to you.

God had always loved me but my heart was so damaged I was unable to receive His love. My heart was like a colander, there were so many holes in it that it leaked love out faster than it was coming in. I learned then that you can't give what you don't have.

I prayed that night that God would give me a new heart and renew His spirit within me. His response was simply, "5:55." I knew immediately that I was to get up the next morning at that time and meet with Him. It became my time to be with my Father which I still do today.

A couple of weeks later, totally out of the blue, Denise came back because God told her to (Thank you, Father in heaven). And every day I get up and met with Him at 5:55 a.m. to praise His name. Now my life's purpose has become to teach others His ways, so they will turn back to Him. Years later Denise gave me a scripture that she believed described my obedience to God calling me to meet with Him in the early morning. At first I kind of "pushed it aside" because it was too overwhelming for me, but then as I read it over and over it really "spoke" to me. Hearing God speak to you is why you need to spend time before God in prayer and reading His Holy word. Here is the verse she gave me:

Isaiah 50:4
The Sovereign Lord has given me an instructed tongue to know the word that sustains the weary. He awakens me morning by morning, wakens my ear to listen like one being taught.

Healing Truth No. 21
Your heart is the driving force within your personality. It is either driving you toward God or it is taking you away from Him.

So Why Do We Need A "Pure Heart"?

1. Our hearts are full of evil from Childhood

Genesis 8:21
Then Noah built an altar to the Lord and, taking some of all the clean animals and clean birds, he sacrificed burnt offerings on it. The Lord smelled the pleasing aroma and said in his heart: "Never again will I curse the ground because of man, even though every inclination of his heart is evil from childhood."

One thing that really upset me before I gave my life to God was the concept of people having a sinful nature from birth. I would think, "*How can a baby have sinned?*" Adults I understand, even teenagers, but babies and young children? This was beyond my comprehension. This was taking "genesis genetics" just too far!

I had trouble grasping this reality because I was looking and evaluating people from a physical viewpoint rather than from a spiritual (God's) viewpoint. Since it is difficult to understand how holy and pure God is, it is also difficult for us to comprehend just how unholy and evil we are. But scripture tells us the truth; we are all born with the sinful nature inside of us. King David understood this when he wrote:

Psalm 51:5
Surely I was sinful at birth, sinful from the time my mother conceived me.

What is called "original sin" is not a choice we make or a belief system we have developed over time. It exists because God told Adam and Eve to obey His word but they refused. They chose to listen to Satan and their flesh (heads, hearts, desires) which resulted in their (and the rest of humanity with them) getting booted out of Paradise.

Only Jesus' sacrifice on the cross removes this spiritual uncleanliness. Nothing you achieve in life can remove it; it is a gift from God because of His love for you. Anyone who rejects this gift (Jesus) rejects God and will remain controlled by the sinful nature operating out of his or her heart. Yes, this is true even for the nicest people on earth. Praise God that <u>anyone</u> who repents can be restored through God's grace!

Romans 3:22-24
This righteousness from God comes through faith in Jesus Christ to all who believe. There is no difference, for all have sinned and fall short of the glory of God, and are justified freely by his grace through the redemption that came by Christ Jesus.

2. The heart you have now is not curable because it is so deceitful.

Jeremiah 17:9
The heart is deceitful above all things and beyond cure. Who can understand it?

The Bible says our hearts are not to be trusted, in fact, it says our hearts are deceitful beyond "all things." This is a pretty strong statement considering how many things are in this life! But when you think about it more closely, it makes sense because only people are deceitful. Surely animals, trees, and plants do not lie—only humans are dishonest. Deceitful means: dishonest, untrustworthy, misleading, cunning, devious, fraudulent, corrupt, greedy, and insincere . . . shall I go on?

Only when God enters your life and creates in you a new, pure heart can you begin to act like Jesus, who had no deceit in Him at all.

3. Your Heart is the Fountain that Poisons Your Personality

Proverbs 4:23
Above all else, guard your heart, for it is the wellspring of life.

Water is essential for all life and for growth. Most natural wells collect pure water in them, because minerals in the ground have already filtered the water. But if something toxic is put in the well the pure water goes bad and poisons all those who drink from it.

Your personality is like a well. What goes into it will be what comes out of it. Worldly pollution in your heart cannot satisfy your thirst for forgiveness, love, and truth, which make up God's spiritual water. Only drinking from God's flowing river of mercy can satisfy you.

Healing Truth No. 22
What comes out of your mouth reveals what is in your heart.

4. Your Mind, Mouth and Behavior are all directed by your Heart

Mathew 15:16-19
"Are you still so dull?" Jesus asked them. "Don't you see that whatever enters the mouth goes into the stomach and then out of the body? But the things that come out of the mouth come from the heart, and these make a man "unclean." For out of the heart come evil thoughts, murder, adultery, sexual immorality, theft, false testimony, slander."

Trying to stop the flow of self-destructive behavior coming out of you without first getting a new heart in Christ is not going to happen. This is because the source of that flow (your heart) is still pumping from a toxic well (your sinful nature). Just like people's hearts keep circulating blood whether they are young or old, tall or short, asleep or awake, or even if they are doing good or evil. So your "heart" keeps circulating compulsive thoughts, feelings, and desires that lead to acting out. A "new heart" is required to stop this circulation of toxic selfishness within all of us.

5. If God doesn't purify your heart Satan will continue filling it with evil

Acts 5:3
Then Peter said, "Ananias, how is it that Satan has so filled your heart that you have lied to the Holy Spirit and have kept for yourself some of the money you received for the land?"

Like Ananias and his wife, many people want to please God, but only after they first please themselves. Again, if the sinful nature dominates our commitment to God it will lead to destruction. Many people say "Jesus is Lord" but only mean it to impress Christians and then say nothing or the opposite when around non-Christians. When "push comes to shove" people often resist God by disobeying His commandments and teachings. Jesus says directly to us, "If you love me you will obey what I command."

When your sinful nature (your flesh) hears this, it laughs and tells you that it's all right not to obey. I learned the hard way that when I believed this lie, not only did I suffer but many others around me also suffered from my selfish, flesh-driven and immoral behavior. I harmed innocent people, may that will never forgive me.

6. You need a new heart from God to fulfill His two greatest commands

Mark 12:28-31
One of the teachers of the law came and heard them debating. Noticing that Jesus had given them a good answer, he asked him, "Of all the commandments, which is the most important?"

*"The most important one," answered Jesus, "is this. Hear, O Israel, the Lord our God, the Lord is one. Love the Lord your God with **all your heart** and with all your soul and with **all your mind** and with all your strength. The second is this: 'Love your neighbor as yourself.' There is no commandment greater than these."*

No human ever born can keep these two commandments without God first creating in them a new heart—one that is controlled by His Holy Spirit and not by the flesh. You cannot keep the Ten Commandments without God empowering you with His grace. And you will never be able to love your enemies, while your flesh rules your mind and your heart. Only with God's grace can any one of us do this.

Healing Truth No. 23
God never takes something bad out of you without, at the same time, putting something good back in you.

7. You need a new heart so you can be filled with God's love, power, and joy!

On August 17, 1975 my wife Denise was lying on a small mattress in the middle of our kitchen floor. She was in great pain and was not very happy with what her body was putting her through. She was delivering Jeramy (our second child) at home, and I was the only "doctor" in the room. Denise had decided early in her pregnancy that she would have her second baby at home, and that I could either help her or stay out of her way. I wisely decided to lend a hand (two actually) in the whole process.

Jeramy was nine pounds two ounces when he came out, and I vividly remember seeing Denise's pain leave her face and turn to pure joy when she first held him. God wants to do the same for you with your pain.

> **John 16:21-22**
> *A woman giving birth to a child has pain because her time has come; but when her baby is born she forgets the anguish because of her joy that a child is born into the world. So with you: Now is your time of grief, but I will see you again and you will rejoice, and no one will take away your joy.*

When you are "born again" into God's Spirit you immediately begin to receive freedom from past pain and deep grief—two of the main roots for depression and self-destructive behavior. By plugging into God's Spirit every day, you continue to be renewed by the Spirit as He cleans out the worthless things in your heart and replaces them with joy, love, and power.
Jesus promises it and I and many others testify that it's true!

Just One little problem: The heart mentioned in the Bible is not your human heart.
The Bible has hundreds of verses that mention the word "heart," but none are talking about the human organ we call the heart. Your physical heart is simply a powerful pump that forces blood throughout your body 24-7 regardless of how you think, feel or live. Your human pump cannot make decisions because it has no intelligence, it does not think.

For example, humans classified as being "brain dead" can still have fully functioning hearts. And the opposite is also true—many people who have high levels of intelligence die of heart attacks regardless of how clever they (and others) think they are.

So what's up with that? It is obvious that the "physical" heart has nothing to do with your "spiritual" heart.

Mark 2:8
Immediately Jesus knew in his spirit that this was what they were <u>thinking in their hearts</u>, and he said to them, "Why are you thinking these things?"

So if your heart is not in your heart, where is it? It's in your mind!

For the heart to have "thoughts and attitudes", it must be in your mind. I believe that the "spiritual" heart mentioned in the Bible consists of all of the following. It is:

1. The center core of your personality
2. The main essence of who you are
3. The total sum of your character
4. The total capacity of your love for the Lord, others and yourself
5. The willingness you have to serve God and others

This heart transformation occurs when Jesus, the living word of God (John 1:1) comes into our hearts and we are born again of the Spirit (John 3:5-6)

Hebrews 4:12
For the word of God is living and active. Sharper than any double-edged sword, it penetrates even to dividing soul and spirit, joints and marrow; it judges the <u>thoughts and attitudes of the heart.</u>

The really good news is that even when you do not fully understand where your heart is, God still does. When you give Him permission to "operate", He scrubs your "heart" clean of all the poisons that have been put into the well of your personality since birth. In doing so, He changes your personality so you can become the person He meant you to be. He created you to be cleansed of the world's pollution.

2 Corinthians 5:5
Now it is God who has made us for this very purpose and has given us the Spirit as a deposit, guaranteeing what is to come.

So What's Love Got to Do with It?

Healing Truth No. 24
God's truth sets you free, but it is God's love (not the world's) that heals you. His love is Jesus.

The world's love (love of the flesh) is called Eros which is where the words erotic (sensual) and erotica come from. It was the name for the Greek god of love whom the Romans renamed Cupid.

Eros is love that is based on sexual attraction and desire. More common terms we use today for this kind of love would be: passionate, infatuation, crush, fixation, obsession, and love addiction.

The world's love is highly destructive because it is "self-centered", it is often referred to as "conditional" love. This kind of human love says, "I will love you as long as you do what I think, give me what I need or want from you. When you don't love the world's way, its "passion" for you dies off and it goes and looks for a substitute. The world through movies, love novels, songs, romance magazines, and the like promote this kind of love.

God's love is totally different; it is called Agape love. God's love is totally opposite from (and opposed to) Eros love, because it is wholly selfless and spiritual rather than physical and self-centered love. Jesus dying on the cross for our sins is the greatest example of God's love. And it is Jesus, who commands us to do likewise.

Luke 6:27
"But I tell you who hear me: love your enemies, do good to those who hate you, bless those who curse you, pray for those who mistreat you."

Regardless of where your heart is, Jesus commands you to love His Father and others with all of it. The only problem with that is that naturally we have no Agape love in us, just Eros love. When we surrender and submit our wills and lives to God, He sends His Holy Spirit into us. We receive Grace which provides God's power to love Him and others by praying and praising God daily (plugging-in). As we let God's love pass through us it kills our natural (fleshly) self and our Eros love for others. If we demonstrate God's definition of love on a daily basis we know we have God's grace at work in us.

1 Corinthians 13:4-7
Love is patient, love is kind. It does not envy, it does not boast, it is not proud. It is not rude, it is not self-seeking, it is not easily angered, it keeps no record of wrongs. Love does not delight in evil but rejoices with the truth. It always protects, always trusts, always hopes, always perseveres.

Reviewing this verse, it becomes quite obvious (if we "think" about it) that our human heart is way too busy pumping blood to monitor the levels of: patience, kindness, envy, boasting, pride, rudeness, selfishness, anger, unforgiveness, evil, protectiveness, trust, hope or perseverance that are in us. These things all come from within our "split brain" thinking.

Healing Truth No. 25
All the "emotional" pain (grief) you feel comes from the right side of your brain where your emotions are located. Submission to God allows Him to wash your pain with His inner peace. While it may not totally go away, you will find a place of "rest" within it.

So how do we plug-in to God's Healing Process?

The steps to God's healing process were presented in the introduction. I call them the "Five Spiritual Steps": 1) Surrender, 2) Submit, 3) Sacrifice, 4) Serve and 5) Stand Firm. Jesus demonstrated each step to us when He was in human form, so that we can learn how to fully connect with God's love which heals all that is damaged within us.

1. Surrender Your Will for God's Will

Colossians 1: 21-23

Once you were alienated from God and were enemies in your minds because of your evil behavior. But now he has reconciled you by Christ's physical body through death to present you holy in his sight, without blemish and free from accusation

2. Submit Your Life to His Purpose for You by Obeying His Commands

Hebrews 5:7-8

During the days of Jesus life on earth, he offered up prayers and petitions with loud cries and tears to the one who could save him from death, and he was heard because of his reverent submission. Although he was a son, he learned obedience from what he suffered...

3. Sacrifice anything Worldly that might be blocking Your inner Healing and Peace

Isaiah 53: 4-5

Surely he took up our infirmities and carried our sorrows, yet we considered him stricken by God, smitten by him, and afflicted. But he was pierced for our transgressions, he was crushed for our iniquities; the punishment that brought us peace was upon him, and by his wounds we are healed.

4. Serve the Lord and others by following His Lead

Matthew 8: 34-34

"If anyone would come after me, he must deny himself and take up his cross and follow me. For whoever wants to save his life will lose it, but whoever loses his life for me and for the gospel will save it. What good is it for a man to gain the whole world, yet forfeit his soul?"

5. Stand Firm against your flesh and you will be free from its slavery

Galatians 5: 1

It is for freedom that Christ has set us free. Stand firm, then, and do not let yourselves be burdened again by a yoke of slavery.

Lesson 4, Prayer Activity 1:   Loving God Enough to Have a Relationship with Him

Life consists of many relationships. Humans were designed to be in relationship first with God, second with self, and third with others. Our relationship with God determines our relationship with our self. In turn, our relationship with our self determines our relationships with others.

If the relationship with God is positive, our chances of having a positive relationship with self-go way up. And if we have a positive relationship with self, our chances of having a positive relationship with others goes way up. Unfortunately, the opposite also holds true.

A. List below your five most important things that you do when developing a positive relationship with someone. (i.e., spending time together).

1.

2.

3.

4.

5.

B. Now list below the five most important things you will do every day to develop a positive relationship with God.

1.

2.

3.

4.

5.

Lesson 4, Prayer Activity 2:   Loving God Enough to have a loving Relationship with You

Thinking of the topics already presented in the book and those listed in 1 Corinthians 13, what are five things you <u>will</u> do to improve your relationship with yourself?

     1.

     2.

     3.

     4.

     5.

Lesson 4, Prayer Activity 3: Loving God Enough to Have a Loving Relationship with Others

Thinking of the topics already presented in the book and those listed in 1 Corinthians 13, what are five things you <u>will</u> do to improve your relationship with others?

     1.

     2.

     3.

     4.

     5.

Lesson 4, Prayer Activity 4: Nailing Your "Broken Heart" to the Cross

Nothing changes inside of you until you ask God to change it. When you go to God and ask Him to help you in Jesus' name, He responds because He loves you and because you are His child. You must be willing to name the things in your flesh that are causing you and others pain and let Him take them, believing (faith in Him) that He can and will heal you. God does this because of Jesus' sacrifice on the cross, not because you (we) deserve it. None of us deserves God's mercy. It is a free gift to us paid for with great pain by Jesus.

Some of the main sources of mental and relationship pain from the right side of your brain (Theater of your Mind) are:

- Memories of being broken hearted.
- Mental videos that keep replaying acts of you being hurt.
- Negative inner voice lies that say you are not a sinner.
- Love Fantasies that always make the pain in your heart go away.
- Deceitful things your mouth says to and about others.
- Bad language that comes out of your mouth (heart).
- Anger and rage that come out of your mouth (heart).

Father God, I have struggled with_____for many years, and it is causing me great pain. Please take it from me by washing my spirit clean from it. Please increase my faith in you Father, in the name of Jesus.

During the next week thank God every day for washing your mind clean, even if your mind tells you nothing has changed, or you feel like your prayer was not answered. Praise God ten times morning, noon, and night for your healing. By your Faith you will be healed, and if you need more faith ask God for more faith.

Deep Healing: Lesson Five

Freedom from Grieving Over Grief

The Light of Scripture:

Matthew11: 29
Come to me, all you who are weary and burdened, and I will give you rest. Take my
yoke upon you and learn from me, for I am gentle and humble in heart, and you
will find rest for your souls. For my yoke is easy and my burden is light.

A Testimony to God's Deep Healing

I've struggled with drugs and alcohol since I was 15 and I'm 58 on my B-day in July
2013. I was raised in a bar in Missouri since I was born in 1955 till I was 16, I hated it.
I had no good parenting skills taught to me. I'm from a very violent childhood and I
stayed in that cycle until 4 years ago.

I was made to go to church from about 5-6 years old. I had lots of hate & resentments
all my life. I thought I knew God on a personal basis, but I was very wrong. I had a
stony heart or cold heart. I knew God and the Bible in my head and not in my heart.

I liked the lesson about the right and left brain. I learned that since everyone has an
inner voice when 2 people are having a conversation there is really 3 conversations
going on at the same time.

Taking this class has helped me heal on an even deeper level. It is very easily
understood.

Thank you,
Leann D.

I just want to add that I do not believe in any way that being a Christian makes us immune or exempt from life's illnesses, sufferings, misery, hardships, violence, persecution, injustice or broken heartedness. Christians get ill, divorced, falsely accused, treated without justice, victimized and die the same kinds of death as non-Christians do. We are humans and we have to learn how to live with deep wounds and pain like everyone else.

Jesus and all his disciples suffered and died, so it will be for every saint (believer) in Christ until Jesus comes again. So why become a Christian? As most humans say, "What's in it for me?"

The difference is that, when true believers (those who plug-in every day to God's power through praise, prayer, service and God's Love) experience the negative forces in life, we do not go through it alone. As believers, God is with us and helps us through the tough times even when others let us down. He carries us and empowers us with His Grace, which gives us the ability to have hope and joy, even while we are experiencing intense pain and grief.

If you have never experienced God's Holy Spirit living in you, the concept (promise) simply sounds like another one of life's major sales jobs. Yet, for those who have asked Jesus to come into their hearts and forgive their sins, the power of God's spiritual touch is more real than anything else on earth. God is more than able to prove himself to you if you really surrender your heart and really submit your will to Him. God does not negotiate terms making individual deals. It is one offer that is for all who will accept it.

Since your life will include misery, pain, grief and death, your only choice is, "Will you live your life with or without God's power in you? Regardless of which choice you make, you will humanly suffer here on earth. The difference in your choice is eternal. With God's power (His Grace) you will never suffer ever again in the endless life after death, which will be the complete opposite if you reject His Love for you while here in this life.

Healing Truth No. 26
God puts His inner peace inside of you, which gives you strength during your suffering.

My wife Denise has been totally healed through faith, while it did not occur on earth it is a reality in heaven. She will never suffer pain or grief again. The only way you will know if this is true is to accept God's terms of surrender and then be overwhelmed with His love for you, a love that no one on earth can ever give you. Without God's love, mercy and grace, Christianity is just another political party looking for votes.

The Sad News about Sadness
God purifying our hearts through lovingly washing our minds and spirits clean of worldly pollution and pain seldom happens all at once. Actually, healing is an on-going, life-long process that strengthens us by keeping us plugged-in to God's power for longer periods of time than if we never had any pain in life. It forces us to our knees, so we can better serve God and others.

We will have mental, emotional and physical pain in life and we will experience human suffering. This suffering often leads us into deep grief. Jesus, while in his human body, experienced deep grief many times. For instance, in the story of Jesus raising Lazarus from the dead Jesus is deeply moved by others suffering and grieving.

John 11: 33-36
When Jesus saw her weeping, and the Jews who had come along with her also
weeping, he was deeply moved in spirit and troubled. "Where have you laid him?"
he asked. "Come and see, Lord," they replied. Jesus wept.

Something that makes grieving so overwhelming is that it is overpowering due to the many negative thoughts (left-side brain) and emotions (right-side brain) that try to drown you in hopelessness. Combined this inner negativity tells you two main lies: 1) you are helpless to change anything that has happened, and, 2) there is no hope for you. Praise God that when we plug-in by faith He comes to our rescue with the power we need to "survive and thrive" through our painful life experiences.

Think of a washing machine that is so overloaded it stops working. When we open it and look inside we realize that it is not working properly because we have too many clothes in it. We are trying to "wash clean" all the dirt out of our lives, if you will, with one washing. Common sense (I know, I know…it is not so common) tells us that we need to take all the wet, slimy clothes out and put them into smaller "piles" that we will clean separately.

The same is true of letting God clean our personalities of grief. We must create smaller **"pain piles"** for His washing with the Holy Spirit. Grief has many different sources and I believe there are different kinds of grief. However you slice it, separating the different sources from each other can assist you in understanding what is causing your current grief. One of the activities following this lesson will help you get started on this process.

Healing Truth No. 27
Jesus suffered spiritually, mentally, emotionally, socially as well as physically.

It is very important to realize that Jesus suffered deep grief from many different sources while He was living in human form. He was not considered attractive, important or respected. Isaiah tells us (Prophesizes) of Jesus' suffering many years before Jesus was even born.

Isaiah 53: 2b-3
He had no beauty or majesty to attract us to him, nothing in his appearance that we
should desire him. He was despised and rejected by men, a man of sorrows, and
familiar with suffering. Like one from whom men hide their faces he was despised,
and we esteemed him not.

Where do our "Pain Piles" come from?

Pain piles can be identified by looking at losses in life that create different types of pain and grief. Here are some examples of specific kinds of pain producing categories that cause deep grieving:

Relationship Grieving Loss of a significant relationship with someone who was a spouse, child, parent, sibling, other family member, friend, partner or co-worker due to conflict and/or tragedy. Teenage romances gone bad, divorce, rejection.

Security Grieving Loss of financial stability, home, employment, ability to work, health and wellness breakdowns such as illnesses and aging deficiencies. Lack of protection for you and/or safety.

Rejection Grieving Loss of acceptance by others (rejection) due to appearance and/or personality characteristics, differences in nationality, race, gender, values and beliefs, lack of knowledge and/or skill sets, and for past social mistakes you have made. Childhood rejection and abuse of any kind.

Failure Grieving Loss of self-respect (shame) due to divorce (parents or your own), arrests, convictions, addictions, immoral acts towards self and others, being fired from work, business failures, not being able to make the "team".

Low Self-worth Grieving Loss of personal value, importance, identity due to extreme self-hatred. Devaluation of self due to negative thoughts, mental images, and feelings about self. Self-rejection due to appearance, lack of ability and failure in life. Grief due to loss of hope for ever having a good life and having a fatalistic life/world perspective.

Addiction Grieving Loss of control over mind, body and life due to self-destructive habits. Deep shame due to having a secret life, lying, deceiving, wasting time and money; doing unhealthy things in your past, present and planning more for your future; hurting others. Being destroyed by what you are addicted to which negatively affects other family members and friends.

Visual Grieving Witnessing extreme acts of violence, brutality, death. Exposing your eyes to extremely graphic images on screens such as the TV or Computer. Reading about horrific details and traumatizing events.

Social Injustice Grieving Loss of security, love and acceptance due to things unrelated to your personality or control. Betrayal by people you trusted who deceive and abuse you with their self-centered actions. Negative worldly and social events that cause great harm to others (and maybe you) and the environment. Bad judges and officers of the law hurting people. School bullying and unfairness among kids, teachers, coaches, bosses. Immoral laws such as abortion and out-of-control crimes like drug sales, human trafficking and child pornography.

Spiritual/Soul Grieving	Loss of loved ones who were ungodly, unrepentant and most likely not saved; Grieving for all the lost souls in the world. Anger at God for any reason; especially for not doing what you wanted Him to do when you wanted Him to do it.

Matthew 23: 37-38 (Jesus Grieving for Lost Souls)

"O Jerusalem, Jerusalem, you who kill the prophets and stone those sent to you, how often I have longed to gather your children together, as a hen gathers her chicks under her wings, but you were not willing. Look, your house is left to you desolate."

Grieving Over Grief (A Grief Cycle)

As a trained counselor, I spent many years listening to people tell me "their stories" which were full of pain, anger and deep grief. I would listen respectfully and respond with empathy, which was very useful and therapeutic at first. Yet I realized that most people tell their stories by bouncing all over their lives, mentioning every person who ever let them down or hurt them.

When people do this, they become emotionally very tired. After many sessions of "dumping" their anger and pain, they can actually become very discouraged because nothing changes. They become experts in "grieving over their grief", which keeps them prisoners of their flesh for more years of their lives. There is no greater grief then wasting life. God is listening, are you ready to take action?

A short example of this happened around twenty years ago when I was in a men's recovery group for over two years. We all shared our "stuff" and then prayed for each other. Each week it was the same stuff and each week it was the same prayers. We genuinely liked each other and laughed and cried with each other every week. The problem was that we didn't change and several men actually got much worse during all of the "laughing".

Eventually several men dropped out of the group and stopped coming, because they felt better when they weren't telling their stuff over and over again. I ran into one of these brothers one day and asked him what made him leave. He pointed at me and said, "You did. The others I expected to ramble on, but you have the knowledge and skills to help us do something different, but you never did."

I immediately got defensive and started rationalizing by telling him that I had been trained to be respectful and as a member of the group I had no right to try and counsel any other member. He hit me between the eyes with, "So who gave you permission not to help us, it wasn't God."

I went home licking my wounds and discussed it with Denise who said, "He's right. God made you to lead, challenge and confront. You were created to help and you do it really well when you get out of the way and let God move through you. Otherwise, you can be very overwhelming and a real pain in the rear end."

I pouted for a week over her "tongue lashing" and then went to my knees and asked God to show me how He wanted me to help those in need. Writing books and teaching classes was His answer. Over the next few years of having me write things down, He showed me how I could help more people in a classroom setting using workbooks than just by passively listening and sitting in a group.

God already knows our stories and wants to help us get free of their control over our lives. Sharing them over and over again with each other does not bring freedom; giving them to God will. All the activities in this book are prayers designed to focus you on God's will for your life. This starts as He heals you, so He can then use you to help others learn to submit to His will.

Listening to those who are hurting and needing understanding is foundational for helping others up to a point. Sooner or later there needs to be a call to spiritual action. In actuality, repetitive talking about problems without taking positive action actually "magnifies" the problems and victimizes the person sharing all over again. People often get stuck in their "stuff" and need a way out, which is why they are seeking help in the first place.

Healing Truth No. 28
You will experience quicker healing when God is in control of your grief cycle, rather than when your (or someone else's) flesh is.

As was stated earlier, a crucial part of the healing process presented in this book is you understanding that **your flesh is not your friend**. You must get power to overcome the damage done to your flesh by other's flesh (and your own), and that power is located in God. The good news is that healing is one of His many specialties, if we only let Him take charge of the healing process. We are healed when we come into contact with His Love (Jesus); not when we sit around talking to each other without focusing on Him as the only solution.

Imagine going in for open heart surgery and after you are prepped and the surgeon starts to cut you say, "No thanks Doc, I will do this operation while you watch." Many of us, over the years, just won't let go of trying to control our lives because we are afraid and do not trust people or God. This is your flesh blocking your healing and refusing to give up control over you. It has no intention of letting you get better. It has more control over you when you are suffering.

When people tell and retell their stories over and over again they are living in the past and avoiding the present. It is like taking all your personality rocks out of your bag (Introduction story) each week only to put them back in so you have something to talk about the next week. It is also like going home and putting all of your "fuzzy little treasures" (Lesson 2) back in your fridge so you have plenty of things to "discuss" the next time you are "entertaining" friends.

Simply talking about your problems is an endless, self-destructive cycle. Your healing can only be found through praise, submission and prayer in the present, the now, today. Healing occurs when we start with God, who knows every detail of our lives, even things we do not know. Only He has the solutions to our pain. But first we must stop grieving over grief, to do this we must first understand the grief cycle (grieving over grief).

Healing Truth No. 29
Swimming through your pain requires Jesus's life preserver, His Holy Spirit.

Running the Emotional Rapids (Cycling through Grief)

Let me start with the fact that there is a negative emotional cycle most people go through when grieving. I call this cycle "running the emotional rapids". It can be very calm at times and super slow only to become very fast and threatening, as you move through the powerful emotions generated by the cycle.

There has been much study about grief in humans and how it impacts personality and behavior. I am not going to try and summarize it all because it would take too long. You can look it up and read more about it as there are many theories, articles and books written on it.

In general, some key points to all the theories are:
1. There are different stages we all must pass through.
2. There is no set length of time for how long each stage will last. Some people pass through the stages quickly and others need more time. And,
3. Having and using support systems such as: understanding family members, friends, good health habits (such as eating and exercising regularly), and participating in support groups with members who have been there before you, all really help speed the stages along.

Basically, the main goal is to experience each stage without getting stuck in any of the them.

This book exists to tell you that God can and will walk through these stages with you, if you want Him to. He is respectful of anyone who says, "Leave me alone." He will honor your request, but He also will help you the second you cry out to Him, in Jesus' name. Sometimes the confusing part is how He goes about helping us through grief. It is never the "quick, take it all away and make everything all better" approach we always expect.

God uses the painful experiences in our lives to shape our character and to strengthen us, so we can help others who are in need and are struggling through their own tough times. He comforts us for His purpose and never for ours. He wants us to become one "family" who care for one another. Unfortunately, the flesh wants us to use each other, to hurt each other, and to fight with each other. Our loving Heavenly Father has all the comfort and healing we need, if we will just ask Him for it and then be willing to help others in His name, after we have been helped.

> **2 Corinthians 1:3-4**
> *Praise be to the God and Father of our Lord Jesus Christ, the Father of compassion and the God of all comfort, who comforts us in all our troubles, so that we can comfort those in any trouble with the comfort we ourselves have received from God.*

God loves you so much that He comforted me and healed me so I would be willing to let Him comfort you (through me) in your time of need. Going through the "rapids of life" will happen to everyone living on earth. Our only choice is whether we let God help us survive the rapids, or go it alone in a leaky canoe called Flesh.

A Quick Look at Ten Stages of Grieving

I am providing ten stages, but in reality there could be just one massive stage or there could be more than twenty stages. No one really knows. Talking about them as separate units, called stages, just helps you better understand the deep, deep impact pain can have on your thinking, emotions, desires, needs, self-worth, and all the other parts of your flesh.

1. Shock, stunning disbelief that leaves you emotionally and mentally crippled.

First, most of us do not see the people or events coming that bring us great pain and suffering. We are usually not paying attention, because we are over focused on what our flesh is focused on. Take any auto accident, mine for example.

Early morning September 1, 1998, while driving to work, I was in a serious accident. It was a beautiful day, sun was shining and the radio was blaring out music, as I moved down the freeway doing about seventy miles per hour. I was a very happy camper until a very large tanker truck, in the lane next to me, hit me and put me upside down in a ditch. My car was totaled, but I survived. Praise God, I had amazingly few physical injuries (whiplash, back problems mostly). Mentally and emotionally was another thing. I was traumatized by the suddenness of the violence and the helplessness I felt, as it was happening. Even though it only lasted a few seconds, it impacted me in a very negative way for years afterwards. My negative inner voice kept telling me that, "Cars are just coffins on wheels."

Even though we live in a very violent world, we just don't expect bad things to happen to us and are shocked when they do. Now for some people this kind of destructive trauma begins at a very early age, with abuse that sadly can go on for years without getting resolved. For others, it occurs later in life, in a random off and on again pattern that confuses them. We hear people often chalking their problems up to "luck", "chance", "it was just my turn" kinds of explanations as to why they were victimized by someone or somebody.

You may have experienced this kind of trauma, often taking you into an emotional state of shock. This very common reaction of "stunning disbelief" may have already happened to you. It may have left you asking, "What just happened to me?" This stage often goes on for a long time because of how hard you were "hit" and how "suddenly". Life's sucker punches that hit us are like that. You may still be walking around, barely functional, but in reality you are emotionally disabled. It is much like going to the dentist; the Novocain (shock) numbs and protects you from the immediate pain. That is until it wears off, and then it really, really hurts.

You just experienced stage one of the "Grief Cycle". Shock is like a morning fog off the ocean that blocks your vision and sense of direction for most of the day. Later it lifts, so you can see a little ways out, only to come back the next morning to find it just as thick. It disables your mind from being able to make simple decisions, so you drift through your day till night comes. Then when you try to sleep, your thinking is too "spaced out" to find the rest you so badly need.

2. Helpless, fear driven questions that "Drive You Crazy".

Stage two begins when shock starts to disappear. It does this so slowly that Fear driven questions start popping into your mind from everywhere. Questions such as:

"What's going to happen to me?"
"What am I supposed to say to people when they want to help?'
"Why is this happening to me at this time in my life?"
"What am I supposed to do next?"
"Who will take care of me?"
"How will I ever pay for all of this?"
"Where do I go from here?"
"Who can I trust now?"

These types of questions are endless and no answer seems to shut them up. Your negative inner voice keeps them coming, so that you feel helpless and think there is no hope. You often are too tired (energy drained) to fight back against this on-going internal dialogue. These kinds of questions often lead you right into stage three which is Denial.

3. Refusal (Denial) to accept what really happened; rejecting your part in maybe causing it.

You come out of the deep questioning stage when you realize that your questions are not going to be answered to your satisfaction. At this point you start to reject what has happened. You blame others and/or tell people it didn't really happen. You refuse to accept it had anything to do with you (if it may have). You attempt to go back to the mental state you had right before the traumatic event occurred. While everything outside of you says it happened you consider it all to be "one really bad dream" that will go away with time.

For instance, during this stage I would sit and wait for Denise to walk through the door at the time she often came home from work. I would do things before hand as if she was going to be there that night. Of course she never came home physically so mentally I would pretend. I would lie to myself that she was on a trip and when I woke up the next day she would be there. Finally reality shook me by the shoulders and I fully realized life would never be the same again. She was gone and I could do nothing to bring her back.

4. Anger at Everyone but You (God, those who caused the pain, the government, etc.).

Once denial will not work anymore you might get angry, really ticked off. You could become so furious that your life drastically changes for the worse. You may alienate others who want to help you or even cause so much trouble at work you might get "fired". You are haunted by the realization that the loss is forever and that you never gave "permission" for anything to hurt you. You never got to "vote" on what happened it just happened. You might even develop a strong urge for revenge. You dream of how you could retaliate, if that's possible, so others have to suffer as much as you are suffering.

You can even get very mad at God for not stopping the event from hurting you. You blame Him for whatever occurred. After all, He could have stopped it because He is God! When this type of thinking and feeling starts to fall apart (and it can sometimes take days or years for this to happen) you can turn on yourself with a fury. Someone has to be held accountable, and if it isn't God or others than it must be you.

5. Anger at Self (and only you).

During this stage, your anger goes inward. Some kinds of depression are rooted in self-hatred, so you sit around feeling guilty, regretful and remorseful that you did not do something you should have done. You start to feel shame for things you did do but should not have done. Combining both negative thought patterns, you end up with all the blame. You are guilty as charged!

In this stage, you believe you were the cause of the trauma that landed in your life and in some ways you might be right. Self-inflicted emotional wounds are very common and while you may or may not be to blame for the traumatic experiences in your life, your negative inner voice tells you that you can never be useful again. When you get to this point in this negative grief cycle, you can become overwhelmed with anxiety that leads you into Stage Six.

6. Loneliness, Emptiness, and "Who Gives a Damn" outbursts.

When the sadness and depression hit bottom, others often distance themselves from you. They do so because they are busy with their lives and because they just don't know what else to do for you. There are some that often stop calling and coming to see you, because they are mad that you have not "snapped out of it" yet. Others give you doctor's names and phone numbers, so you can get some meds which they think will help.

When individuals are suffering for long periods of time they can go in several directions. One direction is violence towards others and the other is violence towards self. Every day there are too many stories of "social shooters" killing others with guns because they are in pain (which is never an excuse to hurt others). Most of them have been writing about their anger and pain for a long time. Many tell others but no one takes them serious enough to turn them in to get help. Sadly, their acts of flesh driven violence create new grief cycles in many others. Those who don't harm others but do end up hurting themselves, sometimes very seriously, are driven to it by feeling helpless in the grief cycle.

7. Overwhelming Sadness, Disabling Fear, and Smothering Depression

Helplessness often breeds deeper levels of sadness, fear and depression. You can become hopeless in your view of your future. You believe life, for the most part, has ended. You become dysfunctional in your relationships with others and your place of work. You often have to (and chose to) stay home where you do not have to interact with others. You isolate in a major way which only feeds your deep sense of loss. You become unable to take care of yourself in healthy ways.

A tidal wave of emptiness begins to wash over you causing deep feelings of being disconnected from not only the world but also from your own life. In short, you begin to just not give a damn about what happens. Your main thought about everything becomes, "What's the point; it will never change what happened." Or, "I don't need them; I can take care of myself!" Things and people begin to lose meaning, value and importance.

At first you try to "ride the negative wave" out but your negative inner voice keeps hammering you with all of its "facts" which magnify your loss into a bigger energy drain than anything you can afford to live with. You might start displaying bursts of rage, verbal tirades, or physically destroying things. You also might shut down and begin thinking of ending your life.

I learned a long time ago in counseling training for a crisis center that, "people who attempt suicides don't really want to die, they just want the pain (grief cycle) to end." Sadly, many people die because their flesh overwhelms them with negativity and pain, talking them into suicide as the only solution.

8. Breaking Isolation: Reaching Out for Help from God and others

It hard to know when it will happen but sooner or later you start to not just go out around people but actually start to talk and interact with them. Often this is with close friends or family who actually insist that you show up to an event such as for coffee, a dinner, a celebration of a birthday, etc.

You really do not want to go but you also are "sick and tired" of being "sick and tired" and you take a chance. It helps take some of the pressure off of you, not all of it, but it is a start in the right direction. Painful questions are mixed in with comments about current events and other people's difficulties. You are very glad when the focus is off of you and all you have to do is eat, drink and listen. Somehow during this stage you realize that there are certain people you can talk to about your pain. While they might not be the exact solution, they often refer you to others who actually can help. It might be a book to read to start with, a video online you can watch or a support class or group that provides a "haven" of understanding from others who are going through the same emotional storm you are.

9. Bursts of Laughter, Sudden Feelings of Relief, Tiny Rays of Hope and then FEAR!

When you start to get stronger and actually feel "like a human being" again the first signs are often laughing at small jokes or things you see others doing. The laughter surprises everyone including yourself but it is a very good release from those powerful, negative emotions you've been stuck in. Laughter is one of the most powerful medicines known for healing from pain and grief. This is often accompanied by moments of feeling relaxed and then relief starts to appear inside your body and as long as you don't over focus on them they continue coming.

After a period of time, tiny rays of hope start to appear. Maybe life can be good after all. Maybe love will come again. Maybe I will find a better job. Maybe I will gain my health and strength back. Maybe I can start exercising again and even listen to music; maybe, maybe, maybe. Then, what I call the "big wham!" happens.

Your flesh has to stop your healing or it will lose control over you so it hits you with strong negative inner voice lies and your theater of the mind plays sad videos to bring you back down into your grief. This kind of relapse can be very normal and is often triggered by external sayings, events or experiences that your flesh uses to take you back into gloom. Remember, your flesh is not your friend which means it is your worst enemy. Its main goal is keeping you from connecting with God's Spirit so you can be healed.

Again, here is another time that you must fight back by kneeling before your Father in Heaven and allowing Him to fill you with His peace. You must feed your spirit and starve you flesh, to get beyond this period in the grief cycle. The flesh only wants to "reopen" your wounds, so you will stay under its control. God wants to give you freedom from your flesh, which brings inner peace even in times of suffering.

10. A new sense of purpose and willingness to return to living and a desire to "clean up" any messes you created during your grief cycling

At this point in your healing process you begin to take care of yourself again; to love yourself by eating right, exercising and interacting with others who understand what you are going through. You sense you have value again and can contribute something positive to others. You take responsibility for those negative things you did while trying to survive the rapids. You repent before God and ask forgiveness from others that you might have hurt during this painful process. You return to life ready for the good things and better prepared for the next round of bad things.

It Takes Lots of Time and Self-Acceptance to Get Through the "Emotional Rapids"

The stages of grief are not sequential but cyclical. Going back to the washing machine concept, all of these stages of grief go around and around and often overlap each other before separating again. Some people have to cycle through the stages several times before they can find release.

All tough situations, especially those that cause us great pain and loss, are also great opportunities to let God strengthen you and use you to help others. I hate the cliché "Let Go and Let God," but sometimes it is all we can do. I prefer a variation on the theme, "Let God and He Will Protect You and Guide You Back to Health."

> **Proverbs 3:5-6**
> *Trust in the Lord with all your heart Lean*
> *not on your own understanding. In all*
> *your ways acknowledge him, And he will*
> *make your paths straight.*

Identifying sources of mental and emotional pain by putting them into "pain piles" allows you to deal with "smaller piles of dirty clothes", if you will. This process is not easy but it is easier than lumping them all together and attempting to receive healing for all past trauma at one time.

God is very capable of healing you all at once (and I pray He does), but often He does it according to His timeline. He does this so that you can learn more about who He is changing you into through the healing process. The process is not the end in and of itself. It is the vehicle God uses to rebuild your personality (character) into the person He intended you to be in the first place. Simon into Peter and Saul into Paul would be just a couple of examples of this type of character development.

To survive the rapids and eventually move beyond them, you need to fully participate in what often feels like the "fight of your life." You need to take Action to counter your flesh! I do believe that there are very powerful and useful things you (God does through you) can do during each grief stage that will help slow down and end the cycle. Here are just a few I might suggest:

Healing Truth No. 30
The river of flesh is too big and it's rapids of pain too powerful for you to try and wade in it. Call upon the name of the Lord and He will lift you up onto solid ground.

Suggested Spiritual Action Steps that Can Help Keep You Afloat

Here are some of the many actions you can take to "help God help you".

1. Shock, stunning disbelief that leaves you emotionally handicapped
- Try not to be alone, have someone who is loving stay with you.
- Plug-in, plug-in, plug-in…let God touch you and hold you.
- Rest often but do not sleep all day. Get outside for walks, do not become a shut-in.
- Take cold showers, they will get you out of your negative thoughts and feelings and bring you back into the "now" so you can plug-in to God.

2. Helpless, fear driven questions that drive you crazy
- Confront your negative inner voice, which always uses fear to hurt you.
- Keep a journal: write, write, write and then burn, burn, burn. Vent negative thoughts and feelings, but don't reread (dwell on) them.
- Don't be around people who keep asking you the same kinds of fear driven questions.
- Join a Christian support group as soon as you are able. There are others who understand your pain.

3. Denial - Refusal to accept your situation for what it really is; reject your part in causing it.
- Ask God for total clarity of the situation.
- Ask God to show you where you may have failed.
- Ask God to help you understand how you may have failed.
- Ask God to forgive you and to turn your negatives into positives.

4. Anger at Others who you think caused the pain (God, individuals, the government, etc.)
- Tell God (not others) who you are mad at (He already knows who they are).
- Pray and then read scriptures on unforgiveness.
- Pray and ask God for mercy and love for those who have hurt you.
- Surrender judgement and vengeance to God.
- Pray for your brother and sister saints in other countries who are in need.

5. Anger at Self
- Talk to God about your failures (He already knows them).
- Read uplifting Christian books. I highly recommend "Jesus Calling"
- Ask God daily for love and mercy for (use your first name) your mistakes.
- Confess self-hatred as sin, you do not have the right to judge God's servant (you).

6. Loneliness, Emptiness, and "Who Gives a Damn" Outbursts
- Do not isolate; find positive brothers and sisters to talk with.
- Don't always talk about your hurts; ask them if you can do anything to help them.
- Do not start seeking another person, a romantic rescuer to energize you. This only leads into co-dependent relationships that will hurt you worse.
- Surrender all plans of vengeance, violence towards others to God and get help.

7. Overwhelming Sadness, Disabling Fear, and Smothering Depression
- PG10X (Praise God ten times for any ten things); repeat as needed.
- Ask God for an attitude of gratitude, so you can focus on the positive.
- Rebuke your fears and helplessness in Jesus' name.
- Read John 4:18, perfect love (God) drives out fear.
- Tell someone if you have any suicidal feelings, impulses, plans.
- Giving up, giving in and quitting to the point of self-abuse will cause pain to others who then will enter the grief cycle. Don't pass it on.
- Eat healthy, let others cook for you, ask others to cook for you.
- Get outside; walk, walk, walk outside where God's creation is tranquil (parks, lakes, etc.).

8. Breaking Isolation: Reaching Out for Help from God and others
- Talk with God daily and Listen in your spirit to what He says. His voice is quiet, calming, peaceful, loving, uplifting and to the point.
- Start reading about how others survived and thrived after similar traumas.
- Keep Plugging-in daily.
- Look in the phone book and online for local support groups.
- Ask professional grief counselors, pastors, friends for help.
- Ask for help with eating healthy and exercising.

9. Bursts of Laughter, Sudden Feelings of Relief, Tiny Rays of Hope, then FEAR
- Ask people to bring you joke books, send you their best jokes.
- Hang out with "laughers", those who laugh often and loudly.
- Watch only positive, funny things on TV-nothing that triggers your grief.
- Use the internet to locate funny books, blogs, etc.
- Praise God for moments of relief and ask Him for more power to turn fear into faith.
- Listen to Christian music (no rock or blues as it feeds the flesh); Sing along.

10. A sense of purpose, willingness to return to living and desire to "clean up" any messes you created during your grief cycling
- Volunteer to help in services to the needy, do not do it alone.
- Go back to work and do not over talk about your loss, your painful trials.
- Confess and repent of things you should not have done while going through the cycle.
- Ask forgiveness from those you might have offended while hurting and angry.
- PG10X, PG10X, PG10X…develop the attitude of gratitude and then use it.
- In God's power keep moving forward mentally, emotionally and physically; keep moving upwards spiritually.

Lesson 5, Prayer Activity 1: Surrendering Your Deep Grief

Grief can consist of any or all of the following: sorrow, heartache, anxiety, depression, misery, sadness, self-pity, bitterness, anger and rage. Use the "Pain Piles" information presented earlier in this lesson to identify your top five areas of grief. Then be more specific about what is the most painful, grief causing issue in that pain pile. Identify and commit to an action for healing.

Example:

Name of "Pain Pile"	Source of grief from that pile.	Action Taken
Relationship Grieving	Denise dying painfully at age 60	PG10X

Name of "Pain Pile"	Source of pain and grief from that pile.	Action Taken

1.

2.

3.

4.

5.

During the next week, take each one of these to the cross and ask God to wash away the grief these situations are causing you. This does not mean that you will become happy these events occurred; just that they will lose their control over you and you will gain spiritual power over the pain.

Lesson 5, Prayer Activity 2: Exposing Your Flesh and Rebuking It

During the grief cycle I firmly believe that the time it takes to run these "emotional rapids" can be reduced (not eliminated) if you let God be in control of your grieving rather than your flesh being in control. Allowing God to rebuke those parts of your flesh (negative inner voice, theater of the mind, fears, worrying, desires, etc.) that are magnifying your pain, rather than helping to heal it, will decrease how long you get stuck in the "river of grief".

Using your five pain pile examples listed in Activity 1, identify below how your flesh is blocking your healing for each one. Then decide if you will ask God to protect you from that part of your flesh through submissive prayer:

Example:

Source of grief	Write how your flesh is using this source to attack you. Denise
(wife for 41 years) dying at age 60	Theater of my mind replaying moments when I said or did things that hurt her feelings.

Write out your prayer here:
Dear Lord, I ask you in Jesus' name to erase those mental pictures in my mind that are condemning me for hurting Denise's feelings during all the years of our marriage. I rebuke them in Jesus' name and thank you Father for your intervention.

Source of grief	Write how your flesh is using this source to attack you.

1.

Write out your prayer here:

2.   **<u>Source of grief</u>**   **<u>Write how your flesh is using this source to attack you</u>.**

Write out your prayer here:

3.   **<u>Source of grief</u>**   **<u>Write how your flesh is using this source to attack you</u>.**

Write out your prayer here:

4.   <u>Source of grief</u>   <u>**Write how your flesh is using this source to attack you**</u>.

Write out your prayer here:

5.   <u>Source of grief</u>   <u>**Write how your flesh is using this source to attack you**</u>.

Write out your prayer here:

Lesson 5, Prayer Activity 3: Nailing Your Grief to the Cross

Nothing changes inside of you until you ask God to change it. When you go to God and ask Him to help you in Jesus' name, He responds because He loves you and because you are His child. You must be willing to name the things in your flesh that are causing you and others pain and let Him take them, believing (faith in Him) that He can and will heal you.

God does this because of Jesus' sacrifice on the cross, not because you (we) deserve it. None of us deserves God's mercy. It is a free gift to us paid for with great pain by Jesus.

Dear Father in Heaven, I come to you in Jesus' name. Please forgive me for being prideful and hard hearted. I want to have compassion and love for myself and others, but just can't seem to do it. I ask you today for Power to love and not hate. I surrender my self-seeking love to you in Jesus' name. Please forgive me for not surrendering control to you over my:

1. Deep Relationship Grieving
2. Deep Security Grieving
3. Deep Rejection Grieving
4. Deep Failure Grieving
5. Low Self-worth Grieving
6. Self-destructive, Addiction Grieving
7. Deep Visual Grieving
8. Deep Social Injustice Grieving
9. Deep Spiritual/Soul Grieving
10. Unforgiveness, keeping records of wrong done to me
11. Roots of Bitterness due to past painful experiences
12. Vengefulness, wanting to get even for being hurt

I cannot do this without your love, Lord Jesus. Thank you for forgiving me of all the things I have done to hurt myself and others. Give me the Grace I need to be more like You and less like me.

I also pray that you will come upon_____(person's name) and call them into your kingdom. I pray you will wash their spirit and mind clean of me that they will not think about what occurred between us (repeat this for each person on your list).

I praise you Father for (name 10 things; anything will do) and thank you for hearing me. I thank you for what I have not yet seen.

Deep Healing: Lesson Six

God is Real No Matter How You Feel

Light of Scripture:

Jeremiah 17:14
Heal me, O Lord, and I will be healed; save me and I will be saved.
For you are the one I praise.

A Testimony to God's Deep Healing

"DEEP HEALING"-- I was sure that I didn't really need to take this course or read the book, since I grew up in a solid Christian home, always felt loved by my parents, married my high school sweetheart, had a good career, and raised wonderful kids. Sounds ideal, but my life was far from it!

My husband and I decided to take the course with Everett and Denise. It was forever to change our lives in a positive way. Although it was easy to take the concepts taught, and apply them to people I knew as a way of understanding them better, I quickly learned that I needed to apply them to myself foremost!!! Reading analogies, like the Ladder Maker, made me realize that I was one of the people in the pit that kept sliding back into it because it took time and effort to "climb" out and to stay out. I learned that "plugging- in" is not a choice if I wanted to stay out of the pits.

Whenever I think I am too busy, or life just gets in the way, I remember PG10X--Praise God ten times!! That ALWAYS gets me back on track and takes my eyes off my situation, and looking up instead. Looking at my husband to change his ways to improve our marriage was not the solution!! I needed to stay connected--"plugged-in"--and allow God to work in me before things could improve at home.

Through DEEP HEALING God worked a miracle in our marriage and I am forever grateful to God and to Everett and Denise, who was obedient to God in writing this book.

THANK YOU!

Phyllis F.

When I was a child I was afraid of basements. They were creepy. I was especially scared when they had lots of stairs that went down into the darkness. I was still afraid even when one of my parents turned on the light at the top of the stairs.

As my parents helped me go down one step at a time, it was hard for me to trust them. They would guide me down holding one of my little hands while I would cling to their side for dear life with my other hand.

My eyes would always be glued to the next step down. I did not want to fall. I was terrified that I would slip over the open side of the stairs into the darkness that was still untouched by the light. I remember that as we descended it always got cooler. The cold air often gave me the shivers. My heart increasingly pounded as we got closer to the bottom, closer to "IT."

I never quite knew what "IT" was but my tiny little mind told me "IT" had to be there. "IT" was waiting to pounce on me; waiting to do bad things to my body. My brain would explode with scary thoughts as I took each step. Even while my parent's voice was telling me, "It is going to be ok; there's nothing down here to harm you," I could hear a louder voice in my mind saying, "Don't you believe it! I'm down here waiting for YOU!"

I would never have gone into the basement by myself. I needed someone else's vision, guidance and power to make the journey into the unknown. I took each step down only because I wasn't alone and knew that they could see the next step ahead of me. They would catch me before I fell.

This book has been written to help you heal from the fear you have of the "IT" that may still be hiding in your personality basement. Part 1 provided the light you need to see by plus the powerful helping hand you desperately must hold to make it all the way down to whatever you must face.

As you work on your healing journey, always remember that you will not be alone—Jesus will be with you. Start with this thought in mind: If the "IT" in your past was really more powerful than you are, "IT" would have already destroyed you. By God's grace "IT" did not, because He has protected you from all the "ITs" in your life and wants to heal you from them.

Healing Truth No. 31
Fear is the root of all worry, fretting and anxiety.

When we worry, we are really demonstrating how much fear there is in us rather than how much faith we have. Faith and Fear are opposites. The more faith in God we have the less fear of the world we will have. Sadly the opposite is also true. The more fear of the world we have the less faith in God we develop. We must choose God or the World, we cannot serve both.

I must mention that Faith does not remove "healthy" fear from our minds. It actually increases our respect for real dangers. Fear of poisonous snakes, severe illnesses or people with loaded guns is a good way to stay alive. But worrying about many others things we cannot change such as: what others think of us, who will invite us over for dinner, and what tomorrow will bring only feeds our flesh and starves our spirit.

Jesus makes this point very clear in His teachings: first we live a life that pleases God and then He will provide what we need (not what the world tells us we need).

Matthew 6:31-33
So do not worry, saying, 'What shall we eat?' or "What shall we wear?' For the pagans run after all these things, and your heavenly Father knows that you need them. But seek first his kingdom and his righteousness, and all these things will be given to you as well.

So How Do We Stop Worrying and Being Fearful?

Great question! Satan runs the world on fear, anger, hatred, and violence which leads to more fear. The simplest way of understanding what God is asking us to do is TRUST HIM. He wants us to know, in our spirits, that He loves us way more than we fear the world.

I have learned how to do this in many small ways which is much better than when I let fear totally control me. What little faith I have comes from reading God's word, and listening to what Jesus tells me about his Dad. From scripture I know that the following are totally true:

- God has more love than we have hate.
- God has more healing than we have wounds.
- God has more wisdom than we have folly.
- God has more solutions than we have problems.
- God has more patience than we have rebellion.
- God has more forgiveness than we have sin.
- God has more blessings than we have curses.
- God has more creativity than we have imagination.
- God has more inner peace than we have inner pain.
- God has more mercy than we have judgement.

I also know that I must not let my flesh be controlled by my sinful nature, the world or Satan. The power of the Holy Spirit does this for me, if I submit to Jesus every moment of every day. When I don't submit I become more fearful, when I do let Jesus be the Lord of my Life I increase in Faith, which always makes fear go down. Remember that Faith and fear are opposites, as one goes up the other always comes down.

1 John 4:18
God is love. Whoever lives in love lives in God, and God in him. Love is made complete among us so that we have confidence on the day of judgement, because in this world we are like him. There is no fear in love. But perfect love drives out fear, because fear has to do with punishment.

The more you plug-in to God the more He downloads His love into you. His love spiritually drives fear out of you, because it is perfect love (Agape Love). We need to trust God.

Proverbs 29: 25
Fear of man will prove to be a snare, but whoever trusts in the Lord is kept safe.

Temper, Temper, Temper

I have a big yard, and the only working outside faucet is on the back of my house. To reach the front yard I have to connect two 100 ft. hoses together so I can water the plants up by the road.

One day I dragged the hoses to the area I was going to water and squeezed the trigger on the water nozzle—nothing came out but a small drip. Getting mad I threw the hose down and marched back down the length of it to find where it was kinked. Of course the hose was fine until I got to about three feet from the faucet on the back of the house where, sure enough, the hose had a kink stopping the water flow.

Still angry I grabbed the hose and started twisting it to get the kink out but the kink soon reappeared about five feet farther up the hose. So then I had to unkink that one which created another one just up the hose and my temper kept increasing to the point where I had to stop and give myself a "timeout."

I learned a long time ago that the best way to deal with my Irish "temperament" was by giving thanks to God. So I stopped, took off my baseball cap and thanked God for the hose, the water, the plants, and for the patience I would need to fix my problem. After I finished "plugging back in," all the kinks (negative emotions) were calmly removed and the plants got watered without any malice in my heart. I am still working on my hatred of weeds.

So it is with your personality. You have many "kinks" that need removing but doing so requires prayer, patience, and practice. It took a long time for those character flaws and habits to be cemented into your character, but there is hope and solutions in Jesus.

Timeout for a Funny: Hard to believe but here is Denise Getting Mad at Everett

Denise's Story called Monster Mohair

In 1974, I decided to knit my husband a camel colored mohair sweater. Even though I was a beginner it seemed like a good idea at the time. We lived in 100-degree weather and I didn't have all the time in the world, since I was busy being a young mother chasing down a little one.

I wasn't a very good knitter and seemed to always be dropping a stitch and taking it out. I hadn't gotten very far along in the project and had been struggling for weeks. One day, in the middle of another unravel my husband asked me, "Are you always going to be knitting this?" Simple question, but it put me over the edge. The mohair tangled, and I couldn't undo it, so I grabbed the whole project and marched into the kitchen. I threw it all in the trash and said, "No, I'm not, I'm making this for you and I see you don't care, so NO I'm not!"

I was so cross with him and frustrated with the knot that I decided I needed to go for a drive. After cooling off 30 minutes later, I returned and decided I better retrieve it from the trash but it was gone! My husband had taken it out of the trash and hidden it in the bottom of his dresser drawer. I was stymied for about 2 weeks as to where he had put it.

When I found it, I put it in my yarn stash and never knitted on that sweater again. A couple of years later I made a cloth doll for my daughter and dolly needed yarn hair. So the finished project of the camel mohair yarn became beautiful doll hair. My daughter Pam still has the doll to this day, after 35 years.

Denise Robinson

PS. The answer to getting a knot out of mohair is to put the project in the freezer for 30 minutes and the knot will easily come out. Maybe I should have done that instead of taking the drive!

Healing Truth No. 32
Anger does not please God, because it gives Satan control over your life.

Ephesians 4:26-29
In your anger do not sin. Do not let the sun go down while you are still angry, and do not give the devil a foothold.

The Flesh Drives Us into Folly

Fantasies (mental movies) are often triggered by negative emotions such as fear, anger, loneliness, depression, jealously, etc. Your flesh then uses these emotional triggers to turn your daily life choices into compulsive, self-destructive patterns. The bible often refers to this as "Folly".

Proverbs 19:3
A man's own folly ruins his life, yet his heart rages against the Lord.

Before we get too far, let me define the word folly as today many people think it is a good thing. Folly stands for: foolishness, stupidity, craziness, madness, idiocy, and recklessness. It also includes silliness, but since I am still working on that one I left it off the list (grin). God tells us very clearly that folly will wreck our lives and fill our hearts with hate towards Him.

Proverbs 5:21-23
For a man's ways are in full view of the Lord, and he examines all his paths. The evil deeds of a wicked man ensnare him; the cords of his sin hold him fast. He will die for lack of discipline, led astray by his own great folly.

Let's be honest. The United States of America is a land of folly. What most people call rights and freedoms God calls sin. We do not have His permission to use our freedom to be immoral, yet the country is becoming more and more so every day. The refusal to demonstrate self-discipline over fleshly demands always brings great pain and sorrow; not just to the person who lacks it, but also to many others who gets victimized by their lack of self-control (folly).

Sin will leave a Bitter Taste in Your Life

Folly (sin) promises pleasure and delivers it for very short periods of time. Then we must pay the real price for sin with suffering. Many of us keep up this negative cycle always blaming others for our decisions to sin. The more we blame the more we stay the same. This type of thinking-feeling-behaving (addiction) breeds a deep root of BITTERNESS that becomes the main block to God healing us. We want the healing, but we also want others to suffer like we suffered. God will not heal us, if we refuse to give up our bitterness.

> **Hebrews 12: 14-15**
> *Make every effort to live in peace with all men and to be holy, without holiness no one will see the Lord. See to it that no one misses the grace of God and that no bitter root grows up to cause trouble and defile many.*

God's grace is the power we need to let God pull the roots of sin out of us, and bitterness is one of the biggest weeds in our personality garden. Life is full of difficult, hard, painful experiences, many of which have nothing to do with our behavior. We often are victims of circumstances, other's acts of folly, and/or spiritual attacks by the evil one. Part of our confusion is summed up in many of our prayers to God when we cry out, "Lord, why is this happening to me?'

God brings and allows hardship in our lives to train us in the way we should go. It is an act of love that most of us totally misinterpret all together. Yet if we embrace God's truths and allow His Holy Spirit to shape our internal character, we end up doing great deeds of service for others. Then not only do we understand how much He loves us, but we also receive a healing inner peace which transcends our fear, anger, bitterness and sadness.

> **Hebrews 12: 7, 11**
> *Endure hardship as discipline; God is treating you as sons. For what son is not disciplined by his father?*
>
> *No discipline seems pleasant at the time, but painful. Later on, however, it produces a harvest of righteousness and peace for those who have been trained by it.*

Healing Truth No. 33
There is no gain without pain, but sadly, not all pain brings gain.

> **1 Peter 4:19**
> *So then, those who suffer according to God's will should commit themselves to their faithful creator and continue to do good.*

God want us to rise above our suffering and do good towards others, so that they will believe that He really exists. Of course, we need God's grace (training) to do this. It is impossible for us to overcome suffering in our own power. We must choose to let God speak through us and to empower our actions, so we can be Christ-like in front of others. We must begin by being Christ-like with our mouth.

James 3:9-11
With the tongue we praise our Lord and Father, and with it we curse men, who have been made in God's likeness. Out of the same mouth come praise and cursing. My brothers, this should not be.

Learning to Love and Forgive Yourself

A major "kink" in your personality hose is not forgiving yourself and others as Jesus has forgiven you. Without this forgiveness, you cannot enter His rest so you can be healed, get your mind right, and receive the grace (power) to do God's will in your life. Forgiveness from God removes this particularly nasty snarl in your "spiritual hose."

When you don't accept yourself for who you are, you often develop a sense of self-rejection. We already discussed how powerful the negative inner voice is and how it makes you feel useless and unworthy. You feel hopeless when you don't like how you look, or how you talk, or how you walk. You even get down on yourself for getting down on yourself; this is the ultimate self-defeating trap! And just as important, you lack mercy for yourself when you have not lived up to others expectations.

Healing Truth No. 34
Sadness (despair) that comes from self-pity and self-condemnation puts you in a front row seat on the Pain-Train!

Your self-esteem goes down, when you won't forgive yourself for the mistakes you make. At these times you don't show kindness and understanding toward yourself, when these are the very qualities you need to improve on the most, so that you don't make the same mistakes again. By not caring for yourself, you then turn to others and hope they will give you the acceptance and nurturing you are so desperate for. This often leads to dependency on others and more hurt, if others can't or won't help you.

Only God can wash away your deep hatred of yourself and replace it with His comfort and inner peace. Once we receive this comfort, God expects us to pass it on to others who are suffering like us. In recovery programs it is often said, "You can't keep it unless you give it away." This is God's expectation for you as you gain His comfort and healing.

So How Do You Overcome Negative Emotions?

Your flesh attacks you with negative emotions like bitterness, anger, fear, depression, discouragement, sadness, and other feelings you experience when you are upset. These negative feelings usually occur because you did not get something you needed (not wanted).

These negative emotions are some of the major causes for acting out (sinning) and must be replaced if you want to be healed.

God wants you to obey His commands rather than follow the demands of negative internal forces inside of your flesh. These forces will only lead you into trouble and shameful behavior. As we learned in Lesson Four, your center for emotional pain is in the right side of your brain. Every one of your negative emotions is directly connected to a negative memory of a negative experience from your past. The more powerful the negative feeling is in you, the more traumatic and painful the experience was in your past.

If negative feelings (flesh) are still controlling you, it indicates deeper trauma inside of you that needs to be healed (washed away) by God. Jesus speaks through Isaiah about letting His power, His Holy Spirit pass through you, so you can be healed. This does not mean you forget what happened or devalue what happened, just that you let God separate you from the flesh controlling you with pain, so you can move forward with your life.

> **Isaiah 61:1-3**
> *The Spirit of the Sovereign Lord is on me, because the Lord has anointed me to preach good news to the poor.*
>
> *He has sent me to <u>bind up the brokenhearted</u>, to proclaim <u>freedom for the captives</u> and <u>release for the prisoners</u>, to proclaim the year of the Lord's favor and the day of vengeance of our God, <u>to comfort all who mourn</u>, and <u>provide for</u> <u>those who grieve</u> in Zion—to bestow on them <u>a crown of beauty instead of ashes</u>, the <u>oil of gladness instead of mourning</u>, and <u>a garment of praise instead of a spirit</u> <u>of despair.</u>*

Isaiah indicates, in this passage, that when we are plugged-in to God and receive His spirit on a daily basis He will provide the following benefits:

- Healing "bandages, casts and crutches" for our disabling misery and depression
- Freedom from internal and external things that control us like slaves
- Release from social and self-made "prisons"
- Relief for over-whelming emotions that choke our hope for the future
- Solutions to our seemingly endless anguish, sorrow and grief
- New, healthy perspectives of God, ourselves and our futures
- Contentment and thankfulness towards God that replaces daily sadness and despair

Healing Truth No. 35
The beginning point of healing is always agreeing with what God says.

Before we can help others with God's power, grace and love, we first must agree with Him that we are poor, brokenhearted, captive prisoner; covered with ashes, full of mourning (deep sadness) and kept ineffective in our healing journey by despair. Agreeing with God is the starting point for your healing, recovery and discipleship.

Once we are in agreement with and obey God's truth we receive forgiveness. Then we must forgive those who have harmed us, especially when they do not deserve it.

Colossians 3:12-17
Therefore, as God's chosen people, holy and dearly loved, clothe yourselves with compassion, kindness, humility, gentleness and patience. Bear with each other and forgive whatever grievances you may have against one another. Forgive as the Lord forgave you. And over all these virtues put on love, which binds them all together in perfect unity.

Let the peace of Christ rule in your hearts, since as members of one body you were called to peace. And be thankful. Let the word of Christ dwell in you richly as you teach and admonish one another with all wisdom, and as you sing psalms, hymns and spiritual songs with gratitude in your hearts to God. And whatever you do, whether in word or deed, do it all in the name of the Lord Jesus, giving thanks to God the Father through him.

Lesson 6, Prayer Activity 1: The Negative Emotion Checklist

Please rate how well you manage (control) each negative emotion (feeling) listed below:

Emotion/ Feeling	I manage It 90% of The time	It controls Me 50% of The time	It often Dominates Me
Anger			
Apathy			
Bitterness			
Boredom			
Confusion			
Depression			
Envy			
Fear			
Frozen Feelings			
Grief			
Guilt			
Indecision			
Loneliness			
Lost			
Lust			
Pride			
Rejection			
Sadness			
Feeling Trapped			
Feeling Unappreciated			
Unforgiven			
Ungrateful			
Unhappy			
Unlovable			
Unworthy			
Useless			

Lesson 6, Prayer Activity 2: Revealing Who Wounded You

Negative emotions often indicate unhealed wounds that were caused by people, including you. If possible, identify up to three people for each of the following pain (wound) categories. Be brief. If you have nothing to write down for a category, leave it blank. These categories are in no particular order. Use relationship names only (such as: God, Mom, Dad, first wife, husband, old employer, past friend, etc.) to identify people not full names.

A. Neglect by another person (being ignored, unattended to, not provided for, etc.)

    1.

    2.

    3.

    4.

B. Verbal abuse by another person (lying, gossiping, criticalness, slander, etc.)

    1.

    2.

    3.

    4.

C. Physical Victimization (physical abuse, rape, beatings, theft, threatened with weapons) by others

    1.

    2.

    3.

    4.

D. Self-inflicted abuse or victimization (acts of self-sabotage, suicide attempts, cutting, over-indulging, destroying relationships, debt, etc.)

    1.

    2.

    3.

    4.

E. Grief due to extreme loss (of loved ones, relationships, jobs, pets, opportunities, health, respect, security)

    1.

    2.

    3.

    4.

F. Physical pain (due to illness, injury, accidents or anything else)

    1.

    2.

    3.

    4.

Lesson 6, Prayer Activity 3: Nailing Your Unforgiveness to the Cross

You have just listed many names and events from when you were wounded by people who harmed you (sometimes unintentionally, sometimes on purpose). God commands you to forgive them in Jesus' name, but saying that does not always make the pain leave your heart. You need to ask God for the power to forgive. Use the sample prayer below to forgive each person you have listed on the previous pages.

Dear Father in heaven, I come to you in Jesus' name. Please forgive me for not forgiving these people, I want to, but just can't seem to do it. I ask you today for power to forgive them, not because they deserve it, but because you have asked me to do it. I surrender my anger and hatred to you in Jesus' name.

I forgive_____for the pain he or she caused me during my life.
I forgive_____for the pain he or she caused me during my life.
I forgive_____for the pain he or she caused me during my life.
I forgive_____for the pain he or she caused me during my life.
I forgive_____for the pain he or she caused me during my life.
I forgive_____for the pain he or she caused me during my life.
I forgive_____for the pain he or she caused me during my life.
I forgive_____for the pain he or she caused me during my life.

I ask you to wash my spirit and mind clean of all hatred and fear of these people. I do not want to continue replaying the violations done to me in my mind. I cannot do this without your love, Lord Jesus. Thank you for forgiving me of all the things I have done to hurt others and myself. Give me the grace I need to be more like you Father God and less like me.

I pray that you will come upon _____ (person's name, if they are still alive) and call them into your kingdom. I pray you will wash their spirits and minds clean of me and that they will not think about what occurred between us (repeat this for each person on your list).

I praise you Father for (name 10 things; anything will do) and thank you for hearing me. I thank you for what I have not yet seen.

Deep Healing: Lesson Seven

I Wants, Gotta-Haves and Gimmie-Gimmies-Gimmes

The Light of Scripture:

Ephesians 4: 17-19
So I tell you this, and insist on it in the Lord, that you must no longer live as the Gentiles do, in the futility of their thinking. They are darkened in their understanding and separated from the life of God because of the ignorance that is in them due to the hardening of their hearts. Having lost all sensitivity, they have given themselves over to sensuality so as to indulge in every kind of impurity, with a continual lust for more.

A Testimony of God's Deep Healing

When I first came to the Deep Healing class, only a few months had passed since my old self had been crushed. Learning to trust God was still very new to me. I had fought for over 40 years with all my willpower from allowing God to be in charge of my life. Being full of pride, anger, and bitterness was "my way" of maintaining control before I surrendered to God.

God watched me try to defeat Satan by myself and escape responsibility by lying, cheating and destroying relationships, because I thought I could outsmart just about anyone. My old self believed I could and would handle any problems better on my own without His help. Was I ever wrong; God knows everything about me.

I finally realized, with the help this class provided, why my old way of coping with stress was my flesh and sinful nature fooling me. My flesh taught me to believe that I was the only person who knew how to protect myself from being rejected and abandoned. This class also opened my eyes to how hurt, rejection, and feelings of unworthiness as a child led to my low self-worth. Fortunately, by having taken the class, I've learned how much God loves me even though my heart was hardened toward Him for so long.

Don't just come to the first class to see if it might help you with your pain and suffering; keep coming back every week until the class is finished. Everett has created materials and ways to help you without shame or being judged by others.

The breakthroughs in my life started happening right away. More importantly I've learned that the early breakthroughs lead to even deeper healing and more fulfilling relationships. When you learn to forgive others (even God) and soften your heart, God can then come be inside you and give you victory over any trial you face. He is truly the only one who can help you win at spiritual warfare. I pray that you want to feel the joy of the Lord because you are one of His precious children.

Blessings,
Steve V.

Summer brings the little beggars out every year; black ants, running around our kitchen like they pay the mortgage every month. Tiny scouts show up first, slowly meandering around looking harmless. They are the ones who are out in front leading the charge. Scouts running ahead of the troops to seek out the best goodies to be had. They are equipped to send out wireless signals to the colony that food is available. The tasters come next, the ones who don't just take a lick or two, but actually dive in for the full sample. They are there to make sure the grub is worth calling out the whole army for. And then the real troops arrive, hundreds of them scrambling all over the counter answering the "bell" for the next round. Soon all of the hordes are "bellying up to the bar" for their fair share of the loot.

Ants are a fascinating species of insects to watch. They are highly organized into large groups of workers, each group having its own assignment for which they are programmed. They travel over many difficult terrains and obstacles to get to their next meal. They are persistent workers who find the food source and after much effort break it down into pieces so they can carry it all back to their family, the colony.

To keep the colony (and more importantly the queen) alive they must transport large amounts of food to the many hungry mouths waiting for it. Their self-sacrificing endeavors keep the colony growing. There is much to admire about the ants drive and commitment to family. But it is this innate drive that leads to its destruction. Ant's tenacity is driven by internal desires. They are programmed by nature to stay alive and multiply, but that same programming also leads to their destruction.

Much like pigs hitting the trough they just can't slow down long enough to know that today's chow is Terro, an ant poison that doesn't kill them until they get back to their colony. Then it kills all who are there. Ants are committed to working hard together to accomplish what is best for their community...dedicated, persistent and loyal. Great team workers, yet they just can't leave that sweet "poison" alone. If it tastes good they just have to ring the alarm for others to "come and get it" so it can be taken back home to their "loved ones".

Humans are very similar to ants in that we are motivated and driven by our cravings, a major part of our inner nature to survive. Most of the time we just can't help it; we must obey our inner demands called "desires, needs and fears". It is these inner impulses that often cause us great pain, because we just can't say no to that "sweet poison" put out just for us. It all seems so innocent at first: texting while driving, a little nicotine, alcohol, and drugs here and a little there; spending money we don't have; sexual contact with multiple partners we know little about; eating as much food as you want whenever you want; risking your health and your body for cheap thrills...what could possibly be wrong with all of that?

The answer is simple: alcoholism, drug addiction, sexually transmitted diseases, diabetes, divorce, lost relationships, family rejection, the loss of jobs, careers and homes; not to mention hospital, court and jail time. Millions of hours of your life down the drain with nothing good to show for it, because you chose to let your flesh and your desires control you.

Healing Truth No. 36
You poison yourself when you let your evil desires unite with worldly temptations that God has specifically warned us to stay away from.

When everything turns for the worse, many people try to shift the blame for their mistakes by asking, "Why is God tempting me? Why does He let evil come near me? He knows I am weak, yet He still does nothing to stop me from making bad decisions." I always answer them by showing them the next verse:

> **James 1:13**
> *When tempted, no one should say, "God is tempting me." For God cannot be tempted by evil, nor does he tempt anyone; but each one is tempted when, by his own **evil desire**, he is dragged away and enticed. Then, after **desire** has conceived, it gives birth to sin; and sin, when it is full-grown, gives birth to death.*

The Power to "Do Don't"

Being a Christian not only appears hard, it is hard! When we read God's word it is full of "don'ts". Don't do this and don't do that…or else! Why should we be surprised, isn't God our heavenly Father? As parents we constantly tell our children DON'T do this or that, because we know it will HARM or KILL them. Yet we still get bent-out-of-shape, because God loves us enough to tell us "Don't" do sinful things that will harm and destroy you. It is even more frustrating when we try to obey his commands in our own power and fail miserably. So how can we succeed?

The power to "Do Don't" is found in God's Grace. Grace is God's love coming into us with such power that it destroys the evil desires inside of you that want to: "mate with evil" and "party hardy" with the world. Obeying God's commands keeps the fire (temptations) away from the gasoline (your desires), so you and others "don't" get burned. Plugging-in to God's power is how you "Do Don't". If this is unclear please reread Lesson One.

Healing Truth No. 37
Only with God's Grace can you Stand Firm against your flesh and the world's temptations. Grace is the power that keeps the two separate from each other.

> **Titus 2:11-12**
> *For the grace of God that brings salvation has appeared to all men. It teaches us to say "NO" to ungodliness and worldly passions, and to live self-controlled, upright and godly lives in this present age.*

A. Grace helps you Stand Firm against Your Evil Desires

Ephesians 4:22-24
You were taught, with regard to your former way of life, to put off your old self, which is being corrupted by its deceitful desires; to be made new in the attitude of your minds; and to put on the new self, created to be like God in true righteousness and holiness.

We often refuse to admit we have evil desires because we call them the, "I wants!" Our wants and desires are always self-centered. We seldom think of others when we are focused on getting our wants satisfied. Our desires are also almost always based on greed; give me more, give me better, give me bigger and give it to me faster! All of this is built into our flesh or what God calls our "old self" or "old nature". When Jesus comes into our lives, we receive God's Grace to "put on our new self".

Now not all wants start out being evil, unfortunately they just take us down roads where evil lives and rules. To get what we want we end up selling our souls to feed our compulsions and over time our gain is PAIN. And when we live in a country that markets and sells to our wants, desires and "gotta haves", we end up with generations full of self-centered addicts who have lost their ability to make healthy, moral decisions. Winning the battle for your mind is crucial, because once you surrender your will to anything or anybody you become its slave.

So whose slave are you right now? If God is not in control of your life, who or what is? Are you satisfied with where your life is heading? Do you see what the end result will be, if you continue doing what your desires command you to do? Is your mind still saying you are in control and can quit anytime you want to? The reality is that most people don't want to quit and/or lack the power to change their unhealthy decisions and behaviors. If this is you, please trust in the Lord and He will heal you and set you free from that which imprisons you.

Galatians 5:16-18
So I say, live by the Spirit, and you will not gratify the desires of the sinful nature. For the sinful nature <u>desires</u> what is contrary to the Spirit and the Spirit what is contrary to the sinful nature. They are in conflict with each other, so that you do not do what you want. But if you are led by the Spirit, you are not under law.

Examples of Evil Desires:

1. Envy/Selfish Ambition

James 3:14-16
But if you harbor bitter envy and selfish ambition in your hearts, do not boast about it or deny the truth. Such "wisdom" does not come down from heaven but is earthly, unspiritual, of the devil. For where you have envy and selfish ambition, there you find disorder and every evil practice.

2. Loving wealth and "other things" more than you love God

Mark 4:19
Still others, like seed sown among thorns, hear the word; but the worries of this life, the deceitfulness of wealth and the desires for other things come in and choke the word, making it unfruitful.

3. Co-dependency (the addiction of control)

People who put other people before God suffer from Co-dependency. This is the addiction of needing to control someone else, because you do not know how to control yourself. Whether you do it with good intentions (you're a pleaser needing acceptance and approval), or with bad intentions (you are a stalker who wants to dominate and destroy) you are still putting your life's focus on a person or group of people rather than God. A key identifier is your interactions are driven by fear and control rather than out of love for the person.

1 John 4:18
There is no fear in love. But perfect love drives out fear, because fear has to do with punishment. The man who fears is not made perfect in love.

4. Sexual Lust (all sexual thoughts and behaviors outside of marriage)

1 Thessalonians 4:3-5
It is God's will that you should be holy; that you should avoid sexual immorality; that each of you should learn to control his own body in a way that is holy and honorable, not in passionate lust like the heathen, who do not know God...

B. Grace helps you Stand Firm against your Body Parts

Even our body parts do not want to serve God, they want to serve self. God holds us accountable for what we do with our body parts. It is so important to Him that we surrender each part to Him. God gives us many bible verses identifying how each part misleads us into sin. It is mind blowing to me that all of these verses were written thousands of years ago, but still clearly describe human behavior today. Let's check a few of these lifesaving verses out.

1. Your Eyes: Be careful little eyes what you see

Matthew 5:27-28
You have heard that it was said, "Do not commit adultery." But I tell you that anyone who looks at a woman lustfully has already committed adultery with her in his heart.

This verse is clear as clear can be, thinking lustfully is adultery. It is also important for us not to use our eyes to judge others falsely. God does not judge us by our appearance (what we look like), but by what is in our hearts and what we actually do. We are not to judge each other any differently.

1 Samuel 16: 7
But the Lord said to Samuel, "Do not consider his appearance or his height, for I have rejected him. The Lord does not look at the things man looks at. Man looks at the outward appearance, but the Lord looks at the heart."

Healing Truth No. 38
Everything you see with your eyes is recorded by your brain into your video-vault.

I loved it when my wife Denise brought up little children's songs of faith from her childhood. I never learned any of them. I was always amazed at how uplifting they were. I will use the main line from one of her favorites to make the next couple of points, it goes like this:

Be careful little eyes what you see
Be careful little eyes what you see
For the Father up above is looking down in love
So be careful little eyes what you see

Time for a funny "eye" story

When I was going to community college, before I met my wife Denise, I went out with a gal who was a knockout from a visual point of view. My roommates could not believe that she had actually asked me to go out with her. They were even more stunned when she drove up in her new mustang to pick me up. Physically she was stunning in every way, but I have to admit that it was one of the worst dates I ever went on; and all we did was go and eat a pizza. Nothing about us matched. Our values, beliefs, sense of humor and goals in life were totally opposite. By the end of the date she didn't look so great to me anymore…nor did I to her…thank God!

There is one funny scene from this strange encounter that illustrates the point God makes about not judging people (or pizzas) by their outward appearance. When we got to the pizza place, she insisted that she would pick the pizza and pay for it. She didn't believe that men should always be the ones to pay and I thought that was an outstanding idea. She went up and ordered and when she came back I attempted to have a conversation with her, since I had never met her before she asked me out. I asked some questions about where she was from, did she have any brothers or sisters, stuff like that and she ignored every question. Instead she kept pointing out other people in the place that she thought looked weird because of how they were dressed.

Before I could comment on her negative views of strangers, the pizza arrived. Now it was very dark in this place, very low lighting and I wasn't paying all that much attention to the pizza when I took my first (and only) bite. I chewed a couple of times and then immediately put what was in my mouth back onto my plate. She just stared at me with her mouth wide open.

I said, "Don't eat it, the olives must have gone bad."

To which she responded, "There are no olives on this pizza, those are anchovies."

I responded in a very surprised tone, "What are anchovies?"

"What …are you stupid, everybody knows what anchovies are," was her kind reply.

At that exact moment, I suddenly found her completely unappealing and unattractive. She ate her pizza while I quietly sat and looked at everyone but her, then she drove me home without a word between us. I was never so glad to get out of a car in all my life and I am sure she felt the same way.

Just one example that our eyes and brains are very misleading and judgmental, leading us into many painful experiences. Remember, just because you think it doesn't make it true. Take the time to find out the "facts" about others before you make decisions about them. Do not be misled by physical (surface) features when God only values what is inside a person's character. Your true character is what you do when no one else is around, what you do when no one sees what you are doing except God who sees all.

2. Your Mouth/Tongue: Be careful little tongue what you say

Ephesians 4:29
Do not let any unwholesome talk come out of your mouths, but only what is helpful for building others up according to their needs, that it may benefit those who listen.

I must confess that I am a talker…one who likes to talk and hear others talk, so this verse has had much value to me over the years. I have gotten myself into many painful situations simply because I said something I thought was useful, intelligent or funny only to find out that those listening didn't see it my way at all. I have hurt many people with things I have said, most of the time without even knowing they were offended by the words I let out of my mouth.

Let's get it clear right here and now, the old saying, "Sticks and stones will break my bones but names will never hurt me" is a lie. Calling people names, making fun of them, and lying are all very painful. And I am ashamed to say that there have been way too many times that I was the one doing the word attack. I knew immediately I was throwing verbal stones and that they were breaking emotional bones. God does not want me (or you) doing this and Praise God that by His Grace I have gained more control over my mouth.

So, if any of you reading this book are one of those people I have hurt with my words please forgive me in Jesus name.

James 3:5-6
Likewise the tongue also is a small part of the body, but it makes great boasts. Consider what a great forest is set on fire by a small spark. The tongue also is a fire, a world of evil among the parts of the body. It corrupts the whole person, sets the whole course of his life on fire, and is itself set on fire by hell.

The Bible has so many verses telling us not to use our mouth to blaspheme, boast, gossip, slander, make false accusations, tell rude and crude jokes, argue, complain, inflict pain upon another, lie, steal, cheat, threaten, or give false testimony about others. I am sure I left out at least ten more important "verbal don'ts", but you get the picture on this one. The list is a long one. Realize that people talk this way for a reason. All this negativity comes from our storehouse of recorded phrases and images living and ruling us from both sides of our split- brain.

3. Your Ears: Be careful little ears what you "listen to"

The key point here goes back to both the negative inner voice and the Theater of the Mind. What we listen to is recorded in our mental sound studio and then used by both of these parts of our flesh to hurt us and others. Lots of poison (Terro for the mind) comes through our ears when we hear things that are not good for us.

One simple example that is very harmful is when children hear adults taking the Lord's name in vain. Since "big kids" do it when they get mad, when they are in awe of something and when they are joking around the "little kids" think it is alright to do the same. The main foundation for standup comedy is often profanity; take away "rude and crude" jokes and most people today would not laugh. And in many movies actors use God's name to damn someone, they say it is more "real" if they talk this way because that is how people talk in real life.

They will be very surprised when they find out that God agrees with them. Every word and action actors say and do in movies is considered "real" by God. His word says they will be held accountable for every one of them. God doesn't recognize "acting" or computer generated fantasy to be "entertainment"… you are what you say and what you do on and off screen.

> **Romans 8:5**
> *Those who live according to the sinful nature have their minds set on what that nature desires...*

Americans think it is part of our "freedom" to be able to curse anyone or anything at any time. Free expression is not free; it comes with a very high price. And that high price comes due when others who are listening (especially little children) repeat what you say, email or text. Like the ants that eat Terro and then take it back home to their nests to feed death to their young, we allow evil into our minds and then take it home and then wonder what is destroying our home "colony".

Words and sounds always penetrate our minds through our ears (HEADPHONES) and leave sub-conscious messages within them. We need to be very discriminating as to what lyrics and words we let into our minds. Advertising and news stations are the same. So many negative things come into our thinking, which build up more negative thoughts and images, and more importantly stress. Much of this negativity drives us into compulsive patterns of acting out in an attempt to reduce stress and pain, but these actions only compound our suffering.

4. Your Hands: Be careful little fingers what you touch

Most, if not all, sin involves using your hands and fingers to some degree. If you give God control over them, you will stop using them to do behaviors that hurt you and others. In short, most of the sins you have been committing will stop. The simplest example is stealing.

Research indicates many workers take things from work that doesn't belong to them. I know I know…you never have…but just in case you are tempted to try it, pray beforehand (no pun intended) that God will take control of your hands, so you don't. Imagine Jesus sitting next to you while you are getting ready to steal something. As one fella told me, "I tried what you said and it was really a bummer…seeing Jesus there totally killed the moment for me dude!" I just nodded my head and said, "Exactly!"

5. Your Legs/Feet: Be careful little feet where you walk and stand

The same is true of your feet and legs. Many people have told me they sinned because they were "in the wrong place."   If you don't walk to places you should not be, you will have a "safety zone" between you and that which is tempting you beyond your control. Let God be in control of your physical movements and the places you go. For example, you can't spend that money you need to pay yours bills if your feet and legs don't take you to the mall where you always buy stuff. Or if you buy them at home from your TV or computer, you can't go online to do so if your feet do not take you into the room where your computer and/or TV are. Self-control requires us to be in control of all our body parts. The good news is that when you let God control you, everything improves and you soon realize that God is full of love for you.

So What Can You Do to Stand Firm against your own Body?

Healing Truth No. 39
You will find mercy, grace and freedom when you need God more than anyone or anything else in this world.

1. Cover yourself with Jesus by thinking unpolluted thoughts

We all need clothes to protect us from outside threats but we also need Jesus to clothe us from inside threats. Are you willing to ask Him to do this? Surrender your mind to Him. He is more than powerful enough to ruin the sinful thoughts that you have been having.

> **Romans 13:14**
> *Rather, clothe yourselves with the Lord Jesus Christ, and <u>do not think </u>about how to gratify the desires of the sinful nature.*

2. Sow Good seed to please the Spirit rather than Bad seed that hurts you and others

> **Galatians 6: 7-10**
> *Do not be deceived; God cannot be mocked. A man reaps what he sows. The one who sows to please his sinful nature, from that nature will reap destruction; the one who sows to please the Spirit, from the Spirit will reap eternal life.*

Are the seeds you are sowing now leading you into eternal death or eternal life? Do these seeds help or hurt your family? Are you in control of what you currently are planting or do you need God's help to change?

3. Praise and Pray to the Holy Spirit for Help

Do you let the Spirit help you according to God's will? Do you realize that the Spirit of God is interceding for you at this very moment? If so then call on Him continually seeking the power that can heal you.

John 16:13
But when he, the Spirit of truth, comes, he will guide you into all truth.

4. Renew your Mind, Get Ready for the Fight, Have Faith

1 Peter 1:13-14
Therefore, prepare your minds for action; be self-controlled; set your hope fully on the grace to be given you when Jesus Christ is revealed. As obedient children, do not conform to the evil desires you had when you lived in ignorance.

The time you spend in God's word will arm you for the fight.

5. See the Big Picture, God's Love for Us Always Rules over Evil

Romans 8:38
For I am convinced that neither death nor life, neither angels nor demons, neither the present nor the future, nor any powers, neither height nor depth, nor anything else in all creation, will be able to separate us from the love of God that is in Christ Jesus our Lord.

In the end you will live with Jesus in His love if you allow God's love to be in your heart.

6. Develop the mindset to Suffer as Jesus Suffered and Praise God for it

1 Peter 4:1-2
Therefore, since Christ suffered in his body, arm yourselves also with the same <u>attitude</u>, because he who has suffered in his body is done with sin. As a result, he does not live the rest of his earthly life for evil human desires, but rather for the will of God.

We have a simple black or white choice; there is no gray area to it. Either we are living for Christ and helping others to find Him or we are living for ourselves and leading others away from God. Which are you doing today?

7. Choose God over your desires and pleasures and He will restore you.

James 4:2
What causes fights and quarrels among you? Don't they come from your desires that battle within you? You want something but don't get it. You kill and covet, but you cannot have what you want. You quarrel and fight. You do not have, because you do not ask God. When you ask, you do not receive, because you ask with wrong motives, that you may spend what you get on your pleasures.

When our flesh controls us through our desires, it is leading us around with a ring in our nose. We talk stupid, we look stupid and we act stupid. We destroy our lives seeking pleasure that maybe lasts a few minutes and then is gone leaving us with a huge cost to pay. And then we do it all over again putting ourselves into a deep moral liability. Instead of being deeply wounded why not accept God's gifts which will free you from the overwhelming pain and shame you have caused for yourself?

Healing Truth No. 40
You can only know what God's gifts are if you accept, open and use them wherever you go.

Lesson 7, Prayer Activity 1: How Much Do You Control Your Body?

Body Parts	I am in Control	I Seldom Control it
Your Left-side Brain		
Your Right Side Brain		
Your Heart/Emotions		
Your Wants/Desires		
Your Eyes		
Your Tongue/Mouth		
Your Ears		
Your Hands, Fingers		
Your Legs/Feet		
Your Physical Energy		

Lesson 7, Prayer Activity 2: What is Your Mouth Telling You?

Pray and ask God to give you the answers to the questions below:

1. What "evil" (negative) things does your mouth say about God?

2. What "evil" (negative) things does your mouth say about you?

3. What "evil" (negative) things does your mouth say about your family?

4. What "evil" (negative) things does your mouth say about Christians?

5. What "evil" (negative) things does your mouth say about healing, this book?

6. What "evil" (negative) things does your mouth say about your future?

Lesson 7, Prayer Activity 3: Nailing Your Desires to the Cross

Nothing changes inside of you until you ask God to change it. When you go to God and ask Him to help you in Jesus' name, He responds because He loves you and because you are His child. You must be willing to name the things in your flesh that are causing you and others pain and let Him take them, believing (faith in Him) that He can and will heal you. God does this because of Jesus' sacrifice on the cross, not because you (we) deserve it. None of us deserves God's mercy. It is a free gift to us paid for with great pain by Jesus.

Some of the main sources of mental and relationship pain that has caused you to not become who God created you to be can be found in dysfunctional families.. Listed below are a few of the things that keep you trapped in pain identified in this lesson. Pray to God for those you want Him to take from you, for example:

- The strongest desires you struggle with
- The lie that "your desires cannot be met by God"
- The lie that "someone else can meet all your desires without God"
- The ungodly things that come out of your mouth
- The ungodly things your eyes look at
- The ungodly things that your ears listen to
- The ungodly things that you love to touch

Father God, I have struggled with_____for many years, and it is causing me great pain. Please take it from me by washing my spirit clean from it; please increase my faith in you Father, in the name of Jesus.

During the next week thank God each day for "washing your mind clean," even if your mind tells you it is still there, or you feel like nothing has happened. This is your flesh trying to stay in control.

Praise God ten times each morning, noon, and night for your healing. By your faith you shall be healed. If you need more faith, ask God for it.

Deep Healing: Lesson Eight

Feed Your Spirit and Starve Your Flesh

The Light of Scripture:

Galatians 5:16-17 (ESV)
But I say, walk by the Spirit, and you will not gratify the desires of the flesh. For the desires of the flesh are against the Spirit, and the desires of the Spirit are against the flesh, for these are opposed to each other, to keep you from doing the things you want to do.

A Testimony to God's Deep Healing

I am very thankful for Everett's willingness to be used by God thru his materials. I have learned the power of Plugging In!

When I feed the "Good Dog" (my Spirit) by Surrendering, Submitting and Praising God the "Bad Dog" (my flesh) loses power over me. Learning how to starve the flesh and feed my Spirit has given me hope and tools for winning the battle I fight every day. Praising God ten times is so easy to do.

1. *Lord, I praise you that you gave your ONLY SON, and LEFT him on the cross to bear my sins.*
2. *Lord, I praise you that you have saved all the love you have ever had for me that I have not received yet, and are now pouring it into my life.*
3. *Lord, I praise you and thank you for the grace my wife has shown me and the value you have given her.*
4. *Lord, I praise you for my wife and the joy she brings me.*
5. *Lord, I praise you and thank you for all my children and the value you have for each of them.*
6. *Lord, I praise you and thank you for our business.*
7. *Lord, I praise you for our employees and the value you have for them also.*
8. *Lord, I praise you for Everett and how you have used him in my life.*
9. *Lord, I praise you for the privilege of living in the United States*
10. *Lord, I praise you for the peace you give me when I surrender and submit and praise you.*

John 3:16 taught me that I am a Diamond, I have great value. I am forgiven. Jesus died so I would know this and be free to do His work with the special gifts He has given me.

LORD I PRAISE YOU!!!!!!!!!!!!!!!!!!!!!!!!!

Mark D.

History Often Repeats Itself

Something deep within you drives you to self-destruct. Something that you just don't understand and thus have difficulty controlling. And it has been around since the beginning of time as indicated by this quote from a famous Greek writer dating back before Jesus was born. This ancient insight illustrates your life and death fight with your flesh for self-control.

> *It is with our passions, as it is with fire and water;*
> *they are good servants but bad masters.*
> Aesop (A Greek writer of fables; 620BC-560 BC)

As you have already read in the previous lessons your thoughts, feelings, passions, desires, fantasies and past experiences will all mislead you into making many mistakes. The truth is: Your flesh is not your friend. It wants what it wants when it wants it. It will nag, threaten, pressure and lie to you until you "feed" it. Most of this book, up to now, has identified things in your flesh that sabotage your morality and judgment leading you into behavior you are later ashamed of. There is still one thing left in you that must be brought into the open. One thing that must be controlled by God's Spirit each day, if you are to be free from pain: your human needs.

Just Like A Barrel Of Monkeys

I recently bought the new BBC video series called "Human Planet." It is a typical high quality production by the BBC High Definition teams who search the world for interesting stories about nature, the environment and people. This particular series recorded 80 different stories about how humans adapt to the environment to survive. Survival dictates that these individuals risk their lives to do amazing things to acquire water and food for a simple existence.

However, one of the stories best illustrates the main point of this lesson, it is a story about monkeys. In a city in India food vendors take carts of fruit and vegetables into the streets every day to make a living for their families. Each cart holds a wonderful array of colors, textures, and smells.

Fresh produce looks so appealing that many people stop and examine each cart's contents. They sometimes even buy things but they do so very quickly. Fear actually grips customers as they stand at the cart and decide what they need and can afford. It is not fear of the vendors or the food that grips the potential buyers—it is their fear of the monkeys.

This town, and many like it in India, worship monkeys (or snakes, rats, cows, or whatever) as gods and believe that they can't harm them or the gods will be angry with them. Unfortunately, the monkeys do not worship human gods and have no qualms about attacking the vendors, customers and carts to steal anything and everything on them. If they were humans we would call them criminals.

On the video the woman trying to protect her produce doesn't have a chance as the monkeys show her no respect. Working in teams some monkeys distract her on one end of the cart while others take food off the other end. She yells at them but cannot hurt them. They know who is in control—and it's certainly not her!

The monkeys behave so badly that they destroy both the cart and her chance to make a living for the day. This goes on every day for all the vendors because of what they believe. This is normal for their town and their culture and it has been so for many centuries. They simply do not see how much their negative inner voice lies are hurting them existance.

Worst of all the monkeys are not only getting everything they want but are also growing in numbers and have taken over the whole town. The monkeys are like bullies in a schoolyard, they terrorize the locals who blame them for everything and take responsibility for nothing. This occurs daily because the locals live by a false belief that justifies their enabling behavior toward the monkeys.

We all live on false beliefs that enable our weaknesses. Beliefs that cause us to feed our internal, self-destructive "monkeys" and we also deny feeding them every day.

"I did not give a banana to that monkey!"

Your human "needs" are like pesky monkeys who do not respect what you think or believe. They are empowered and fed by getting what they "need" to feel satisfied. Like the monkeys, even if they are satisfied one day they always come back the next to continue their attack upon your life.

Self-control requires that you master your needs rather than letting them become your masters. This is not easy to do, in fact without God's Holy Spirit it's impossible to do.

All people are born needy and not much changes as we grow up. A need is something you must have to continue living, to feel safe, secure, loved, accepted and valued for what you do. Your needs can be placed into five categories all which start with the letter "S."

1. Survival needs are things you need to stay alive, thus making them the most important: water, oxygen, warmth, shelter from severe conditions, any kind of food supply, protective clothing, reproduction; etc. These needs make daily demands that must be met, if you are to live another day. The goal of these needs is your **Life/Physical Survival**.

2. Safety needs are also powerful. Besides surviving, you must also grow healthier over time. This includes things such as clean water, a regular place to live, regular meals with wholesome food, cleanliness, time to sleep without threats to your person, and protection from things that could hurt you. The goal of these needs is your **Health/Growth Survival**.

3. Social/Love needs come next: attention, acceptance, belonging, friendship, play time, cooperation, learning, communication, being understood, validation of efforts and achievements, obtaining intimacy and interpersonal harmony. The goal of these needs is your **Relationship Survival**.

4. Success needs would include: achievement, recognition, power, independence, challenge, financial security, respect, having and understanding relevant facts, and creativity. The goal of these needs is your **Ego/Self-worth Survival**.

5. Spiritual needs would include: salvation for human sins; understanding spiritual realms, trusting God (faith) to meet all your needs, being one with your Creator so that your needs stop dominating your decision making, and seeking and obeying God's laws. The goal of this need is your **Eternal/Spiritual Survival**.

Needs Often Mislead Our Minds, Taking Us down into Darkness

If you cannot control your needs it will be very difficult for you to control your morality. In God's Word, the Bible, morality is often referred to as Light and immorality as Darkness.

God is very clear in His Word about what is acceptable and what is not acceptable. In our society, we call doing the "right" thing moral and doing the "wrong" thing immoral. For example, if I pay money for food I have ordered I am being moral (an honest man) and if I steal the food without paying for it I am immoral (a thief).

Unfortunately, our society has too many different manmade definitions and lists as to what is right and what is wrong. It seems to change every year, if not every week, due to popular demand. Having rejected God's commandments and spiritual laws we now live by situational ethics or "majority rules" morals. If the mainstream of America says something is moral then it is socially acceptable (i.e. abortion, sexual immorality, lying, stealing, etc.) even if God condemns it.

Of course when your needs go unmet for a continued period of time your concern for right and wrong goes downhill faster than when your needs are being met. It only makes sense that being moral is much easier when all your main needs are being consistently met. For example, if your physical need for food is being met you will be less likely to steal than if you are starving.

When needs are not satisfied on a consistent basis your moral right and wrong take a back seat to whichever set of needs is being satisfied the least. In short, whenever you are really needy you are most open to temptations that promise to meet your needs, even if only for a short period of time and at a very high price. Need demands often cost us self-respect, friendships, jobs, marriages, and money we cannot afford to waste, but do it anyway because an inner need tells us to do so.

Healing Truth No. 41
Whatever you need the most is the weakest part of your personality; it is where you are the most vulnerable to be manipulated by your flesh, the world and Satan.

Greed for the Need

It's pretty common knowledge that you can catch monkeys by putting something they really like to eat in a bottle. The food object has to be the right size to just fit through the opening and the bottle has to be tied to a stake in the ground.

When the monkey puts his (or her) hand into the bottle and grabs the object his fist becomes too big to pull his hand back out. He could be free to run away immediately if he would just let go of the object; but he has decided it is his and he will not give it up so he is caught.

This is where the self-abuse illustration comes into play. When baited by a temptation that meets one of your biggest needs do you refuse to let go and become trapped by your own "greed for the need?" All of our bad choices in life occur this way.

Compensating for unmet needs starts in your mind (enemy #1). When you get bored with just thinking about it you then go into the world (enemy #2) to see what will satisfy your hunger. Then you are faced with Satan's (enemy #3) temptations which provide the opportunities to act out in ways that meet the need. The best way to win this war is by "mastering" your flesh so it does not respond to the world's baiting which places you in Satan's traps.

Through fantasy most of your Theater of the Mind Productions are aimed at meeting needs you cannot get met in reality. Your mind generates all kinds of visions and "pain free" relationships where you always end up satisfied and successful. In these fantasies, you direct your mental images (memories) to end up different than what actually happens in reality. Your perception thus is that you come out a winner rather than a loser.

Unfortunately, the more you view these "movies" the less you appreciate reality when you have to come back and live in it. You can fool yourself for short periods of time but overall you cannot keep up the charade forever.

Let me be perfectly clear that dreams are not always bad things. Let's say you have always wanted to fly a plane and have dreamed about doing so for years. One day you pay for a flying lesson and actually fly a plane—that's cool. It is cool because you are not harming yourself or any others. You are not doing anything immoral.

Compulsively acting out, be it with food, sex, alcohol, drugs, or whatever else, is always abusive because it is harmful (painful) first to you and then to others. Dreams that lead you into such acting out are "poison" in your mind and in your decision making.

Consequently, whatever you need the most is the area where you are the most open (vulnerable) to being manipulated by immoral people and situations. For instance, if you have a high need for security you may do immoral acts (embezzlement, prostitution, steal cars, etc.) to get money. Or you may marry someone you do not love who has money and will financially take care of you.

Once your strongest need is met your next strongest need will take over your decision-making. For instance, using the last example, if your highest need is intimacy and you found someone you are not married to that you want to be intimate with you might not get a divorce from the one who is providing you with money, as it might cost you security (your 2nd highest need). Adultery often functions this way, and in many societies "flings" are considered moral (socially acceptable, "everybody is doing it" type of dysfunctional decision making) when it is really nothing more than rationalizing to let your flesh (monkey) get what it needs.

Needs and Fears: Opposite Ends of the Same Monkey

Needs and fears are reverse ends of the same "monkey". Every monkey has a head and a tail located at opposite ends of their bodies. Another good illustration is found by examining a coin—one side is "heads" and the other side is "tails." While the two sides look different, they are still part of the same coin. If you know what one side of the coin is (your need) you will also always know what the opposite side is (your fear).

Needs make human behavior move toward objectives—yours are always motivating you to attempt to gain something. That is how they get "fed." Fears are also motivating but they motivate you away from (not toward) people and/or objects. The stronger your need is the stronger the other side of that need (its opposite fear) will also be.

For example, if you have a high need for respect you will also have a high fear of being disrespected. So you behave accordingly, doing anything to gain the respect of others so your fear does not come true. You avoid (fear) any situations in which you might lose others respect.

To continue, let's not focus on basic survival needs such as water, food, etc., instead let's review some of the more powerful human needs and their related fears that often lead us into trouble. Mark any in the following short list that you know negatively influence your decision making and behavior.

High Need for:	Strong Fear of:
Acceptance	Rejection, ridicule, criticism
Being Understood	Not being listened to, opinions not valued
Independence	Being dependent on others for anything
Intimacy	Being alone, living life by yourself
Achievement	No opportunities to accomplish, achieve
Control	Being controlled, dominated by others or situations
Power	Being powerless in any situation
Harmony	Being in high-conflict, anger-filled situations, criticism
Organization	Being in chaotic, unorganized and unclean environments

A very interesting and useful insight is that while everyone has the same needs and fears, not everyone has the same preferences (strength of importance) for those needs. Like values, what is really important (a strong need) in one person's life could be totally unimportant (a weak need) to someone else.

This is often true in marriage where opposites often attract each other. If the husband's needs are very different than the wife's needs, the marriage relationship usually is filled with extreme stress and conflict as neither one places the same value (importance) on their spouse's primary needs.

A very common pattern I have seen in marriage counseling is the wife has a high need for intimacy (fear of being alone) while the husband's highest need is for independence (fear of being dependent on anyone for anything). These two conflicting needs help explain why she gets upset at his spending fourteen hours a day working and only coming home to eat and sleep. She can become insecure and bitter because he (his behavior) is not meeting her strongest needs (companionship, communication, and romance). With him being gone for so long she could end up finding another man who has her same high need for intimacy. Once she realizes that her new friend is more interested in her than her husband is the immorality door is opened and the marriage has been damaged. People are addicted to the internet because they can find anyone they need to meet the need they have without having to be in a "real" relationship.

Her husband, on the other hand, enjoys work because he can be his own boss. No one is putting demands on him but himself. He works long hours because he wants to be good at what he does but also because he is afraid of having to go home where he knows his wife is waiting for him. Once there he is subject to her comments (expectations, criticisms, demands, sobs, etc.) which make him feel like she is trying to control him. His fear of being controlled motivates him to go to work early and to stay late. He feels okay with this pattern because he is not involved with another woman but he doesn't realize that he is actually having an "affair" with his job.

The opposite can be just as true, where it is the woman who is the "workaholic" and the man is the one who needs intimacy. Either way, when needs clash between people conflict stirs. And conversely, where conflict occurs there is a clash of primary (strongest) needs. In short, it becomes one big monkey fight. In this kind of situation both partners are responsible for their own "pets".

Healing Truth No. 42
Monkey see, monkey do. If you don't want to act like a monkey don't hang out with them.

All of your inappropriate behavior is learned. Somewhere you first saw someone else do what you are now doing to hurt yourself. We all learn new behavior vicariously (through sight, vision) like children do watching older humans do things. We learn through contact and imitation. This is what makes movies and the Internet so powerful. We don't even have to know who the actors are to want to copy their attitudes, movements, and actions. The "If they get to do it why can't I?" mentality very quickly teaches bad habits to good kids.

For example, a young child who loves being accepted for who he or she is, will be drawn toward (and most likely mimic) same sex adults who demonstrate how to get accepted by others. The more similar the need preferences are between the actor and the viewer, the more likely the "Monkey See, Monkey Do" reality will follow.

Advertising uses this approach by hiring superstars to hawk their products. Young kids want to be like that superstar so products sell at very high prices. We've seen tennis shoes go from $20 to over $200 a pair just because some social superhero's name is on them! This happens so easily because of the flesh-world-Satan connection. When we do not have the Holy Spirit inside of us to protect us from this evil partnership we soon submit and succumb to our monkeys and give them whatever they demand no matter what it costs us and others in doing so.

So Which One is Your Chunky Monkey?

The more you let your needs dictate your decisions the less happy with reality you will be. Obsession is simply your body telling (demanding) you to get what it wants "or else." Somewhere, somehow, you have to stop letting your needs control your behavior or you will sell yourself to the highest bidder.

The biggest bully in the "needs barrel" is what I call the "Chunky Monkey." This need is the strongest one in the pack, the main agitator that insists on being fed the most every day. *When you let God take control over this bad boy you will notice a significant decrease in your stress and an instant increase in your joy.* It will also help you surrender the next monkey in line.

Healing Truth No. 43
Joy brings you inner peace while seeking happiness often leads you into habitual suffering.

There is an important difference between joy and happiness. Happiness is related to the Greek word for "happening." Happiness is temporary and related to what is occurring in the moment. So if you call a woman to ask for a date and she agrees you are happy, but if she says no you are unhappy. Or if your boss gives you a raise you feel happy but if he denies you the raise you feel upset. This resulting feeling—positive or negative—indicates that you controlled by external, immediate circumstances and behaviors which is indicates you are a "dependent" personality type.

On the other hand, *joy is long-term contentment that comes from your overall outlook and attitude* <u>toward life based on God</u>. Joy is determined by "internal" beliefs and values rather than by external people and events. People who have great joy do not enjoy going through negative circumstances but they don't let the circumstances emotionally control them either. They are considered "independent" personality types. When we choose to rejoice in the Lord always and let Him meet our needs our Joy goes way up even if external events are not pleasing or rewarding.

An excellent example of this is found in Acts 16:16-34 where Paul and Silas are "stripped, beaten, and severely flogged" for casting an evil spirit out of a slave girl. Then they were thrown into prison where the jailer put them in the inner cell and fastened their feet in the stocks. Now I would be crying, yelling, screaming and throwing a fit but Paul and Silas continuously praised God, prayed for others and sang hymns. I am sure they were not happy about the circumstances but they did not let it rob them of their joy in the Lord. Their spirits were much stronger than their flesh.

Oh yes, read the rest of the story…the jailer and his whole family ended up giving their lives to the Lord because of the men's demonstration of great joy in adverse circumstances.

A good way to remember and apply this spiritual truth is realizing that JOY stands for Jesus, Others, and You. Your joy will increase when you put Jesus before others and others before yourself. When you base your life on happiness you will always be controlled by your strongest needs. Measure your life by how much joy (not happiness) you have and then you will know who's in control of your life—God or your "Chunky Monkey."

Now here is where the "negative inner voice" will lie to you. Before I surrendered my life to Jesus, I thought I would never be happy (get my needs met) if I became a Christian. I believed my negative inner voice which kept telling me that Christians were boring and never had any fun.

I also wanted to acquire many of the pictures that were in my Theater of the Mind and to make those fantasies real I needed to do "unchristian" things. My "Chunky Monkey" got fed so much that he turned into King Kong and began dismantling my life. Instead of having joy in life, I became stressed, sad, fearful and needier. Feeding needs makes them bigger, stronger and more demanding "beasts".

When I surrender my needs to God on a daily basis they stopped pestering me all day long. So what happened to calm them down? I surrendered them to God who in turn gives me power (GRACE) to control them. I trust in Him to become my provider.

> **Philippians 4:19**
> *And my God will meet all your **needs** according to his glorious riches in Christ Jesus . . . All the saints send you greetings, especially those who belong to Caesar's household.*

God's Holy Spirit came into me and took control over my flesh with all its weaknesses. God, who understands everything about me, filled me with His love which satisfies my needs. The emptiness inside me left and now I am not as quick to want to copy other humans destroying their lives. Instead, I want to copy Jesus honoring God and helping others in need instead.

Healing Truth No. 44
God can provide abundantly more than what you need. In contrast, the world only offers "smoke and mirrors": illusions of approval, false love, cosmetic fulfillment, and fake tranquility if you take the right pills.

It is sad when people who call themselves "Christians" have no intentions of ever being like Jesus. They don't study His life or His teachings. They do not intend to surrender their wills to Him or obey His commands. Yet these same people still think God will bless them regardless of how they live.

If this is you I challenge you to leave this way of thinking and to take God's offer of help. His free gift of His Holy Spirit is for everyone who wants it; let Him meet your needs. By doing so you will be healed and set free of any and all "monkey business." He will change you from a pagan into a true child of God.

> **Luke 12:29-31**
> *And do not set your heart on what you will eat or drink; do not worry about it. For the pagan world runs after all such things, and your Father knows that you need them. But seek his kingdom, and these things will be given to you as well.*

Unfortunately your needs will make you put things and people before God.

To increase your healing you must understand that you (and everyone else) create images (fantasies) that are designed to satisfy unmet needs (desires) in your life. This simply means that when reality lets you down, you will go into fantasy to get your needs met.

There are many images you might use to do this. Three things people often choose are: entertainment, relationships, and work. Let's briefly define and examine each.

1. Entertainment: Sports, travel, music, movies, Internet, hobbies, reading, crafts, etc.

Example:

Hollywood creates a fictional, dysfunctional situation with most of its movies. What it calls entertainment, has become an addiction for anyone who is dissatisfied with life. Scripts are carefully written to meet unmet needs, showing dialog with images that will connect with whatever is missing in your life. Even people out of work who can't pay their bills still have time and money to be entertained. Movies are just one illustration. There are so many others such as boats, cars, vacations, clothes, eating out, hobbies, sports, video games, etc. When you spend all your human energy being entertained (or entertaining), you lose connection with God.

2. Relationships: Marriage, friendships, team members, work associates, clients, teachers, customers, students, coaches, etc.

Example:

People who are needy (and that would be all of us) look most often to other humans to meet their deepest needs. They get involved with others because they hope the relationships will satisfy their needs every day. But these needs are seldom fulfilled, because humans are limited as to how much they can give others. When needs don't get fed quickly enough, people often grow tired of the relationship and change it, like exchanging a dirty shirt for something more fitting.
After a while, when that relationship has run its course, they move on again.

This reality is captured by the phrase, "What have you done for me lately?" This reoccurring desertion and abandonment destroys all involved, especially the kids who are left in the dust. In short, God is not impressed when any of us let the world meet our needs instead of letting Him meet our needs.

3. Work: Job related skills and talents, careers, occupations, jobs, schedules, visions, purpose, goals, challenges, resources, training and rewards

Example:

Many people strongly believe that who they are is what they do for a living. They believe their jobs determine their worth in life. Their work becomes their identity, and when the job ends, as all jobs eventually will, they have great difficulty. All their conversations go back to when they were doing this job or winning some performance award. Their needs are so enmeshed with their work that they lack an identity separate from it. So work demands their attention over their families, their friends, and even God. Surprisingly, pastors often fall into this category. Often they will experience very negative outcomes (i.e., burn-out, failed marriages, rebellious children, loss of faith) over time.

Healing Truth No. 45
God is Reality. Thinking anyone's flesh will make you happy is fantasy. Let Jesus crucify your monkeys (sinful nature, self, thoughts, needs, fears) before they crucify you.

Galatians 5:24
Those who belong to Christ Jesus have crucified the sinful nature with its passions and desires.

You are either feeding the flesh or feeding the Spirit, you cannot do both at the same time. And if you think you don't feed either you are really feeding the flesh. Laziness, apathy and lack of concern are signs that your flesh is controlling your life. Most men I meet in this state are joyless and unhappy, often blaming their emptiness on others and events. If this is how you are living it does not have to be that way.

God has all the love required to meet your needs. His love can fulfill your needs if you let Him control your life. He does this through relationships with other Christians; by placing you in situations that best fit your skills and talents; and by placing within you a deep gratitude for all that you have, even if you don't have much. *In God's kingdom, love brings contentment and security.*

Healing comes as you
feed your Spirit and
starve your
"Monkeys".

Lesson 8, Prayer Activity 1: Identifying your Strongest Monkeys

Listed below are 21 primary needs that we prefer to one degree or another. You have 10 minutes to circle your top 5 needs, and then rank them 1 (most) to 5 (least) in order of importance.

Acceptance: To be accepted for whom you are without having to do anything. To be allowed to think, dress, and behave as you want to, when you want to. To be liked by many people. To feel like you belong to a group. To have many friendships.

Achievement: To set and reach specific goals within specific timelines. To accomplish difficult tasks. To be able to move into situations requiring more difficult skills. To be allowed to produce quickly and efficiently.

Appreciation: To be acknowledged for being thoughtful and considerate. To be valued for being a hard and reliable worker. To be given this acknowledgment and value without having to ask for it.

Attention: To be able to hold people's attention when speaking. To maintain eye contact with people. To be in front of crowds for speaking, entertaining, and athletic performances.

Challenge: To be pushed to your fullest point of development. To dare to attempt something that others think can't be done. To take risks within the environment for profits or for thrills.

Creativity: To be allowed to create with ideas and abilities. To be able to express creativity without rigid structures or timelines. To have variety in what you do and when you do it. To have support for the expression of all creative energies.

Harmony: To live and work in a friendly, safe, and quiet environment. To have emotional stability within personal relationships. To have few conflicts with others. To not have to fight for your rights as an individual.

Honesty: To be told the truth no matter how bad things are. To not be lied to, even if it is meant to protect you. To be able to say what is on your mind without fear of retaliation. To not be cheated or deceived by others. To be able to trust someone with all that is important to you.

Independence: To be able to do what you want to do when you want to do it. To be allowed to be alone when you choose to be alone. To be able to work without interruption on projects of your choice. To be able to live, work, and play where and when you want to.

Intimacy: To be close to individuals on a personal level. To be able to trust someone with your innermost thoughts and emotions, and for them to trust you with theirs. To be like "family" with people. To have one-on-one time for introspective discussion.

Organization: To have an orderly environment. To be able to work with systems that are logical and sequential. To be able to provide structure to non-structured situations. To be rational about how things are done.

Play Time: To be able to tell jokes and laugh with others. To organize and enjoy parties with others. To be allowed to create entertainment for others. To have time to play games. To be able to do whatever pleasures you. To be able to relax doing what helps you unwind.

Power: To be able to control situations and events. To be able to cut through obstacles and adversity that steal productivity time. To acquire money, status, and position for influence.

Recognition: To be praised for what you have created or accomplished. To get verbal thanks and credit for work done. To have your name written in a place where it will be read by many people. To be promoted or honored for new ideas and work efforts.

Respect: To be thought of as knowledgeable and competent in a specific area. To be admired for what you think, say, and do. To receive the required personal and professional regard and honor due your role and position of authority. To receive credit for the work you do.

Responsibility: To be given accountability for important tasks in important situations. To have the authority to make decisions without having to ask others.

Safety: To have safety guards that protect you and loved ones from physical and emotional harm. To work and live in non-threatening environments. To be able to trust others not to be physically aggressive with you.

Security: To have few financial debts. To have few major changes in life. To know your job is secure. To have a warm home and food in the house. To be able to take care of health needs. To be able to provide for children's necessities.

Spirituality: To have communication with God, a relationship with Him that gives you the power to complete His will for your life. To have inner peace that comes from being in communion with His Holy Spirit.

To Love: To be able to nurture and care for others in need. To give rather than to receive. To share what you have to help those who have not. To create safe and warm environments for family and friends. To do for others, being thoughtful and considerate of their needs before your own.

Understanding: To know how and why things are the way they are. To be able to get specific answers to questions. To be able to teach others what you know. To comprehend what you are being asked to do before you have to do it. To be allowed to share and use your perceptions of situations and others to make things better.

Your Top Five "Chunky Monkeys" Are:

Monkey 1: _____

Monkey 2: _____

Monkey 3: _____

Monkey 4: _____

Monkey 5: _____

Lesson 8, Prayer Activity 2: Needs and Fears are opposite sides of the same coin

Needs are very strong motivators within our personalities. We have strong individual preferences for certain needs while others are less important to us. Some individuals have a high need for **attention** and love to have people watching them while others, who have a low need for attention, feel uncomfortable when people focus on them. People who have a high need for security tend to be low risk takers while high risk takers tend to have a lower need for security and a higher need for challenge.

Need Rule No. 1: You spend more time and energy trying to get what you need the most and much less time and energy pursuing your weaker needs. If you have a high need for intimacy, you will put more effort into trying to obtain this need than if it is low on your list.

Need Rule No. 2: What you fear the most is opposite of what you need the most. For example, a very high need for **acceptance** means a high fear of **rejection**.

Need Rule No. 3: Whatever you need the most will be your most vulnerable area. People can manipulate and mislead you easier when they meet your strongest needs. Because of this your strongest needs are intertwined with "emotional triggers."

These triggers (external words, behaviors or situations) release powerful emotions (internal feelings) that cause you to behave in dependent ways. For example, if you have a high need for respect you will get very angry (emotional) when someone is being rude (trigger) to you. If they then continue you might explode and verbally or physically fight them (act out) to prove to them that you deserve respect. Gang members often turn to violence because of their need to be "respected." By acting this way they demonstrate that they are being controlled by (triggered by) "disrespect." They (like all the rest of us) are servants to their own needs.

Please list your top five needs from Activity 1, what the opposite fear would be for each need, and then what emotional triggers are related to them.

Example: Need = Challenge   Fear = Boredom   Trigger = Routine   Emotion = Depression

Strongest Needs	Biggest Fears	Triggers	Emotions
1.			
2.			
3.			
4.			
5.			

Lesson 8, Prayer Activity 3: Nailing Your "Chunky Monkeys" to the Cross

Nothing changes inside of you until you ask God to change it. When you go to God and ask Him to help you in Jesus' name, He responds because He loves you and because you are His child. You must be willing to name the things in your flesh that are causing you and others pain and let Him take them, believing (faith in Him) that He can and will heal you. God does this because of Jesus' sacrifice on the cross, not because you (we) deserve it. None of us deserves God's mercy. It is a free gift to us paid for with great pain by Jesus.

Some of the main sources of mental and relationship pain come from growing up in dysfunctional families. Listed below are a few of the things that keep you trapped in pain identified in this lesson; pray to God for those you want Him to take from you, for example:

- The negative inner voice that lies saying that your needs come first.
- The strongest five needs your flesh uses to control you.
- The strongest fears you have related to your strongest needs.
- The lie that you can get all your needs satisfied without God.
- The lie that someone else will meet all you needs without God.
- Emotional triggers that hook you into self-destructive patterns that feed your flesh and starve your spirit.

Father God, I have struggled with_____for many years, and it is causing me great pain. Please take it from me by washing my spirit clean from it. Please increase my faith in you Father, in the name of Jesus.

During the next week thank God each day for "washing your mind clean," even if your mind tells you it is still there, or you feel like nothing has happened. This is your flesh trying to stay in control.

Praise God ten times each morning, noon, and night for your healing. By your faith you shall be healed, if you need more faith ask God for it.

Deep Healing: Lesson Nine

We Don't Protect What We Don't Value

The Light of Scripture:

1 Timothy 2:1-5

I urge you, then, first of all, that requests, prayers, intercession and thanksgiving be made for everyone-for kings and all those in authority, that we may live peaceful and quiet lives in all godliness and holiness. This is good, and pleases God our Savior, who wants all men to be saved and to come to knowledge of the truth. For there is one God and one mediator between God and men, the man Christ Jesus, who gave himself as a ransom for all men-the testimony given in its proper time.

A Testimony of God's Deep Healing

I cannot thank you enough for the Deep Healing class and your dedication.

I was raised in a dysfunctional home and was thrilled to become an adult and get far away from what damaged me. I basically slapped on an emotional Band-Aid, participated in some surface counseling, and convinced myself I had walked away unharmed. Deep down I knew I was not healthy, and I struggled with a very negative inner voice but I kept on.

Three years ago I lost my 36-year-old brother to a drug overdose and the floodgates opened. My brother had been an addict for many years; I believe in order to dull the pain from our childhood. When I lost my brother my emotional Band-Aid was ripped right off. I still didn't have the skills or knowledge to heal, and I was angry with God. I had known my brother was an addict, and I had prayed for him daily asking God to please heal his addiction and the pain behind it.

When God answered my prayer by taking my brother away, I was devastated. I have been suffering for three years feeling separated from God and in deep pain over the hurts of my life that damaged my siblings and me. For three years I became more and more depressed. I medicated using food and avoided facing the real pain that was chasing me. In this state I discovered your class.

I felt as if the lessons each week were written just for me. Not only did I hear the message of God's love for me—which I so desperately needed—but I also heard some of the tough truths about my behavior that I needed to hear and be accountable for.

I will take this class again when it is offered. I have been so richly blessed each week. I physically feel lighter and more hopeful than I have in years.

Although it is hard and dirty work, I am removing the pig poop to reveal the diamond God intended me to be. I am so incredibly grateful to both of you.

Michelle D.

There's Diamonds In That There Pig Poop!

As I looked out at the healing class I saw many faces covered with shame and lack of hope. I asked the class, "How many of you feel like you are really nothing more than a big pile of pig poop?"

Surprised by such a statement many slowly raised their hands not making eye contact with me.

I continued by saying, "Growing up many of you had people throwing pig poop on you so often that you learned how to throw it on yourself. And then you started throwing it on others even those you cared about. Now you believe, based on what has happened to you in life and what you have done in your life, that there is no hope for you. You think you are far beyond getting clean, far beyond getting healed. You believe you are worthless and unlovable."

All eyes in the room were now on me. Perhaps many were thinking I would pick out certain ones and tell them to leave, that it was too late for them. Others were afraid I would tell them they were so messed up that even this class couldn't help them. As I paused and looked around the room I became aware that what they were thinking would kill them if I did not help them by bringing the lies in their heads out into God's healing light.

To begin this long process I wrote John 3:16-17 on the board leaving spaces where it says the words, "the world."

For God so loved_____that He gave His one and only Son, that if_____believes in Him, he or she shall not perish but have eternal life. For God did not send His Son to condemn_____, but to save_____through Him.

I then asked them to write their first name in the spaces and to read it again. As they did I randomly pick out one name from the class and wrote it in the spaces in the verse on the board.

For God so loved Jayne that He gave His one and only Son, that if Jayne believes in Him she shall not perish but have eternal life. For God did not send His Son to condemn Jayne, but to save Jayne through Him.

Healing Truth No. 46
God values you so highly that He sent His Holy Spirit to wash the pig poop off of you so you can have the love and life God intended you to have.

I then told the group the "good news," that while humanity was totally covered with pig poop (sin, hurt, pride, fear, greed, lust, and all the rest of it) God sent Jesus to die in our place. Jesus paid for our sins with his life so that we could be forgiven, healed and washed clean forever. God gave what He valued most, His Son, for us because He values us so highly. I added that God is not coming back for anything on earth but our souls and spirits . . . not for plants, not for animals, not even our bodies—our souls and our spirits are the only things He values on earth.

Yes, you are still covered in pig poop but Jesus wants to restore you. He wants to clean off everything that is poisoning you (and those you love) if you will let Him. Jesus suffered a horrible death and gave His life for you because He loves you. Anyone who says otherwise is a liar, including your own mind.

Ah yes, here is where your negative inner voice and theatre of the mind show up again. They tell you and show you why you are nothing but pig poop. They go on and on listing all the bad things that have happened to you and all those bad things that you have done. They show you pictures of you sinning over and over again; and many times you are enjoying every minute of it. A major lie in your head is that you are nothing but pig poop and you always will be.

While we all get covered with pig poop (sin) in life God still sees what is deep inside, what He created us to be before the world polluted us—and that is a DIAMOND. Healing is God pressure washing the pig poop off of (and out of) us. This takes time. It is often painful. The poop on us has been there for a long time. Yet when He is done we are so clean that, just like a diamond, we sparkle and reflect light God's light so others can see God's mercy.

Healing Truth No. 47
The "Pig Poop" from your past is the fertilizer God uses to feed and grow your future.

> **2 Corinthians 1:3-5**
> *Praise be to the God and Father of our Lord Jesus Christ, the Father of compassion and the God of all comfort, who comforts us in all our troubles, so that we can comfort those in any trouble with the comfort we ourselves have received from God. For just as the sufferings of Christ flow over into our lives, so also through Christ our comfort overflows.*

Another miracle is that God will not only wash the pig poop off and out of you but then He uses it in your life to help other people. People who are struggling with their flesh think they are all right when, in fact, they are suffering from pig poop saturating their lives.

God takes your "lemons" and makes lemonade because that is one of His specialties. It is how He teaches you to be Christ-like and then it will become your testimony so you can encourage others in their journey back home to God. I am an example of that, when I was covered in pig poop I sinned in ways that deeply damaged other people. I never believed I could be forgiven let alone used to help heal people. That is God's signature sign of His love for us, he uses broken failures in life to bring his message of hope to other broken failures in life.

As God removes the pig poo you begin to understand what it is like to have inner healing. You feel lighter, more hopeful and definitely more loved. Every testimony in this book is telling you how God cleaned the pig poop out of those brothers and sisters. As you read their statements you can see the Diamond shining in them. When you let God do this you will see others needs and hurts as more important than your own. You will develop a testimony of how God can and will help those who reach out to Him because He healed you. While life is still difficult you will no longer feel alone on your journey, and more importantly, you will have changed direction and are now traveling toward God rather than away from Him.

This journey is life long and doesn't happen quickly for most people. Some people are healed immediately and I have total faith God can and does do that for certain people according to His will. But I know that healing often takes longer to happen for most people, so we learn discipline that comes from hard work. Once down the trail, we become "scouts" for those who are to follow. To learn your lessons quickly you must surrender your entire mind to God. Notice I did not say to a church, an organization, or a person…but to God who is the only one who can prove to you that everything I am writing is reality.

Stinkin'-Thinkin' is Pig Poop in the Brain

As I previously stated, a major block in receiving God's love and healing is self-hatred. You cannot receive His love if you hate yourself (and most of us addicts do). The roots of self-hatred are lies that are often referred to in recovery as "stinkin' thinkin'." These lies are full of hate that tell you each day that you are unforgiveable and of no value to anyone. These lies first tell you it is all right to sin and then criticize and damn you for doing so!

God will remove the lies in your thinking but first you must be willing to give them to Him; to surrender what you have believed for years to be your one true friend. You see, the biggest lie your brain tells you is that you can only trust your own thinking when, in fact, your thinking is what harms you and others the most. God can and will change your negative thinking towards you, when you trust Him enough to let Him care for you.

> **1 Peter 5:6-7**
> *Humble yourselves, therefore, under God's mighty hand, that he may lift you up in due time. Cast all your anxiety on him because he cares for you.*

Healing Truth No. 48
Your relationship with God determines your relationship with yourself, which in turn determines your relationships with others.

Life Is All About Relationships

The relationship you have with yourself is the oldest, most personal and intimate relationship you will ever have. You can never escape yourself. Even after death you are still with you, just not in your current body.

In this life, you spend 24 hours of every day with you. Only *you* will ever live inside your skin. The old saying, "Where ever you go, there you are," captures this obvious truth.

So if you do not like who you are, if you do not love who you are, if you mistreat yourself the time you spend with yourself will be very unsatisfying. You will be filled with loneliness, unhappiness, anger, and fear.

The human way of dealing with this is to find things outside of the body to make up for what's going wrong inside the body. This explains compulsive self-destructive behavior completely. You try to make the internal pain go away by medicating with external stimulants such as: acting out with alcohol, drugs, food, shopping, gambling, codependency, sexual immorality, etc. Of course, these things only make the internal pain disappear for a short time at a great cost to your mental, emotional, and physical health.

The crucial fact is that the relationship you have with yourself *dictates* all the relationships you will have with other people. If your relationship with yourself is negative, that negativity will poison the relationships you have with others. It does this by seeping out of your personality through your speech, your opinions, your insecurities, your anger, your fears, and your uncontrollable need to control the people you say you love.

The relationship you have with yourself is controlled by your brain. Your thinking (positive and negative) starts in the brain, creating decisions on how you should act. If you cannot control your thoughts, you cannot recover from that which controls your behavior.

If your mind says you are pig poop, and you believe it, you will devalue yourself and act accordingly. Doing this leads to loss of hope and self-hatred. If your mind says you are valuable, because God says so, you will act accordingly. The main challenge is: how do you change a negative thinking pattern into a godly (positive) thinking pattern?

The answer to this question lies in understanding what we often call, "Self-Worth."

Self-Worth **(SW) is the measure of the overall valuation a person makes about himself or herself.** It is the deepest level of relating or greatest intimacy individuals can have with themselves. SW functions like a personality battery that provides energy to live life. When it is low there is less energy (pessimism) and when it is high there is more energy (optimism). Our chances of success in life greatly increase when we have higher energy.

At birth your SW battery is empty. Humans are not born with self-worth and it is not inherited. It is learned (programmed) by many interactions with family, friends, co-workers, and other significant people who influence us while we grow up.

The key to improving your low SW is accepting that what is learned can be unlearned. While self-worth is very difficult to humanly change it is very easy for God to change. To better understand how it can be changed; let's look at how God created self-worth to be "two sides" of the same coin.

Each side of the "self-worth coin" strongly influences personality and behavior patterns, but in different ways. Each one is equally important in understanding how your personality and behavior are determined and changed. The two sides of the SW coin are called: **self-concept** and **self-esteem.**

A. *Self-Concept* (SC) is the cognitive relationship you have with yourself.

When you have relationships with others you *think* about them in many different ways. For example, you constantly are having thoughts, ideas, assumptions, judgments, and perceptions about people you meet.

You have made thousands of evaluative thoughts about me just from reading this book. The same is true regarding your relationship with yourself. You go through these same mental processes when relating with who you are. Your thought processes about you determines your SC level (a measure of how high or low your SC is). High SC is healthy, low SC is unhealthy.

As we have read previously, your thinking actually speaks to you inside your head...this is called self-talk. This "inner voice" inside your head can be positive or negative, often it is both. For example, when it tells you to do things that are healthy, such as eat good foods, it is positive. But when it tells you it is okay to do unhealthy things, such as shooting heroin, it is extremely negative.

Your inner voice (IV) operates within your self-concept greatly shaping how you comprehend things. When your IV is positive you see reality for what it actually is; but when it is negative you have a distorted view of reality. The more negative your IV is the more lies you believe, the more fear controls you, the more depressed and sick you become, and the less hope you have for the future. You actually have your worst enemy living inside your head telling you things that will destroy your body and your relationships.

An example of this would be jealousy. People who suffer from this character flaw always have a strong negative inner voice. It tells them they cannot trust the one they say they love. They cannot trust that person because their thinking lies to them telling them the other person is going to hurt them. Believing this internal lie they become angry and aggressive and often do things to hurt the other person first. This destroys the person they say they "love."

Your Identity Is Who You "Think" You Should Be

Self-concept is where your identity comes from. Your mind tells you (through your inner voice) who you are and that you should act accordingly. We call this identity. Similar to a movie script where you have to play a part in the movie and have to look and talk a certain way to be successful, in reality your identity tells you how to act in life so you get acceptance. Unfortunately, this is often based on lies that are interwoven into your mind by negative inner voices (yours and others) so you try to be someone you were never created to be.

In the healing process, God reframes your identity to help you understand what your true purpose is in life. Purpose always follows identity. If your identity is flawed then your purpose will also be off course. You will be using up your time and energy in life trying to be someone you were not meant to be and trying to accomplish things you were not meant to accomplish.

Healing Truth No. 49
Self-hatred is a major personality weed that is rooted in low self-esteem. God must pull it and replace it with His love if you are to have inner healing.

B. *Self-Esteem* (SE) is the emotional relationship you have with yourself.

Esteem means to respect someone, to hold him or her in high regard or honor. Besides thinking about (analyzing) yourself you also have feelings about and toward yourself. The emotional side of your personality (mind) contains your feelings and emotional reactions to self. Just like when you emotionally react to other people's personalities and behaviors, you also have similar reactions to your personality and behavior. An example would be you have negative feelings toward critical people, but you also feel negative about yourself when you are critical of others.

A key component of self-esteem is that it is a measure of the level of love and friendship you "feel" toward yourself. In short, it indicates how much you "like" who you are and reflects how much you accept yourself. When their SE is low, people reject themselves with disgust and they are not "friendly" toward their existence. This means they make very bad decisions about taking care of their bodies and their lives.

Also, they resist attempts from others who try to convince them they should treat themselves better. They have no mercy for themselves when they are sick or emotionally down and heaven help them if they ever make a mistake because they will not forget or forgive. They are their own worst enemy.

People with low self-esteem have such a lack of regard for who they are that they disrespect their thoughts, feelings, bodies and lives. This is a sign of deep embarrassment and disgust about their personality. This self-devaluation is most often driven by deep, painful shame and self-condemnation.

> If God waits until after you die to judge you
> why are you condemning yourself now?

Understanding the Differences Between Guilt, Shame, Conviction and Mercy

Guilt (left-side brain conviction) logically says you deserve to be punished for having done something wrong or for not doing something right that needed to be done.

Shame (right-side brain damnation) is emotional rejection of self (negative feelings) and makes you feel unforgivable and unlovable for being who you are. It says you will always be "wrong" and should never be forgiven or loved.

Conviction is God spiritually touching you to let you know that you are going in the wrong direction and/or are doing something immoral (sinful). It is a warning of his judgement if you do not repent (stop going in that direction and confess) and obey His commands.

Mercy is God lovingly forgiving you for your wrongs and not giving you what you deserve.

Riding the Shame Train Produces More Pain for You and for Others

Shame is one of the biggest chains keeping you bound to a life of pain and compulsive acting out patterns. Shame is the root system of self-hatred. It feeds it and keeps it growing within your personality. You cannot love someone if you hate him or her. God wants to remove the hate from your heart toward others and yourself so He can use you. God will remove your shame for the things you have done and for the things that others have done to you if you ask Him. Until it is removed you will continue riding "The Shame Train."

The Shame Train's destination is always darkness; anyplace where you can hide from others and, hopefully, yourself. It speeds your life into self-destructive relationships, practices and situations. This shame train runs on pain, your pain. Each car on the train is full of memories, full of hurt and embarrassment. Each car is full of pig poop, which repulses others. No one wants to ride this train with you. You believe you have a one-way ticket and can never get off until it plunges into the abyss. Nothing can be further from the truth.

Praise the name of Jesus! Because He died for your sins (shame acts included), you can be taken off this train and never need to get on it again. Does that mean you don't have to be held accountable for all the bad things you have done? No, it doesn't. You must allow God to take you off the train and scrub you clean so you no longer live in the pig poop of your past. This scrubbing often requires you to make amends for the wrongs you have committed, but by doing so you not only get off a train full of pain but you also gain freedom and power to live the life you were created to live.

None of this happens until you let God heal both your self-concept (your left-side brain relationship with you) and your self-esteem (your right-side brain relationship with you). In doing so God heals your mind and fills it with His truth. In short, you start riding the only train that is heading "home," and that is the "Glory Train."

Healing Truth No. 50
You can't keep God's love unless you give it away to others.

God commands you to love your neighbors, *as you love yourself.* The more you reject yourself, the worse you will then treat others. The more you love yourself as Jesus loves you, the more you will let God love others through you. It is a free gift to them and to you.

Remember the garden hose illustration. God wants to pass His love, like water, through you to others so they can grow. This spiritual watering is what makes marriages and children grow healthy. When you are plugged-in the Holy Spirit passes through you empowering you to bless others with His mercy, healing, wisdom, teaching, and grace. While God's love is passing through you to others you are getting healed regardless of how they respond to His outreach. When you have "personality kinks" in your hose you keep His spirit from flowing through you to them. God considers this disobedience. God created us to function properly but our own choices and willfulness often keeps us inoperative and defective in helping others experience God's love.

The prayer activities in this book are all designed to help take those "kinks" out of your personality.

Lesson 9, Prayer Activity 1: Increasing Your Self-Worth

Please circle the Self-Concept and Self-Esteem steps listed below where you need to improve to be healed:

A. Steps for Increasing Self-Concept (Left-side Brain Healing)

1. Surrender your mind (will, thoughts, mental images) to God daily.

Nothing powers your human battery (your spirit) quicker than giving God your will, which is an act of plugging into His Spirit. When you do this, His grace strengthens you and gives you the wisdom you need to get through life's challenges.

2. Accept God's identity for you rather than the one the world gave you.

God created you for a purpose. Your identity in Christ and your spiritual gifts are to be used to help others, so God will be glorified.

3. Identify and confront what your negative inner voice is telling you.

Listen to your inner voice and decide what is not honoring to God. These thoughts will harm you and others, if you continue letting them influence your life. Confront them using God's scripture.

4. Praise God…especially when you feel worried, depressed or angry.

Thanking God (praise) is another way to plug in and drive negativity out of your head. God is light, and when you plug into Him, His light comes into you.

5. Protect your relationships by checking your thoughts before you speak.

First you think, then you decide, then you act. Your thoughts will often set you up for failure, and you won't even know it. Making decisions based on lies will mess up your relationships. Protect them by letting God heal your mind.

6. Value yourself and others based on what Jesus says and did for you, not on what you (or someone else) can do in this world.

Your individual worth should never be based on appearance or performance levels, only on what God says about you. No one is ever worthy of God's love, but your spirit and soul (not your flesh) are still highly valued by Him.

A. Steps for Increasing Self-Esteem (Right-side Brain Healing)

1. Praise God daily. Thanking Him for everything you have really feels good.
This time of praise pleases God and He, in turn, will bless and energize you.

2. Ask God to give you strength and a clear memory.
Ask and you shall receive, seek and you will find. God is reaching out for your hand to help you up from your misery and despair. When you accept His help, your mind will be healed and you will remember what you need to give Him.

3. Don't trust your emotions.
Emotions (feelings) are part of your flesh and often mislead you. Remember, God is real no matter how you feel. Do not let emotions make decisions for you or you will be sorry.

4. Forgive yourself and others as God forgives you.
When God forgives you of something that you have confessed, it is a sin to continue hating yourself for it. Have mercy on yourself, as you would on a best friend.

5. Improve your level of friendship (mercy) with you.
Self-esteem is a direct measure of how much you like yourself. Knowing who you are now, would you pick yourself as a best friend? If not, identify why not and change so you can receive God's love as well as give it.

6. Understand the difference between your guilt and shame.
Guilt (left-side conviction) says you have done something wrong. Shame (right-side damnation) says you are unforgivable and unlovable for that wrong. Guilt says you deserve to go to jail while shame says you should never get out of jail. Let God wash you <u>spiritually</u> clean, restoring your ability to receive His love.

7. List all shameful things you have done and that have been done to you.
Ask God what He would have you write down. List things using ranges of time (see activity 2. Do not leave this list where others can find it. Protect yourself and keep it private.

8. Confess these shameful things to God in front of someone trustworthy who will pray with you and keep them confidential.
Have an accountability partner (or partners). Sharing with others who can keep what you say confidential helps to drain the pain that comes from shame. Ask God for wisdom to know whom you should share and pray with.

9. Sing songs of praise. Listen to Christian music that lifts up the Lord's name.
Feed your spirit by turning off music and movies that poison your relationship with God.

10. Don't be in the wrong place, with the wrong people, doing the wrong things at the wrong time.
You need God's love and acceptance more than you need acceptance and approval from others, especially those who will harm you more than love you.

Lesson 9, Prayer Activity 2: Healing Your Five Trails of Shame

Shame = Overwhelming feelings of disgrace, dishonor, disgust and self-hatred.

Steps To Remove The Shame (Poison-Pig Poop) from Both Sides of Your Brain.

1. Very Important!! Pray for God's guidance and protection as you go down each trail.

2. Turn off the negative inner voice. Do not let it stop you from getting healed by telling you lies. It's time to take care of your business with God.

3. List all offenses in each category (trail). Divide them according to age categories: 0-5, 6-10, 11-15, etc. Identify who was harmed and what each offense was.

4. Ask God to forgive you and to "wash your spirit clean of shame" with each offense in each category. Take them to the cross and leave them there.

5. As you pray over each act, ask God to heal all people involved wherever they are. Remember Jesus said in Luke 23:34: "Father, forgive them, for they know not what they do."

6. Burn your lists when done. Do not re-read them, giving the negative inner voice power to attack you again with the same old lies. Reading them just puts the lies back into your mind. Repeat this process as often as you need to.

7. Remember that Jesus sacrifice "washes us clean of shame", when we believe and confess. Trust Jesus for you healing.

Romans 10:9-13
That if you confess with your mouth, "Jesus is Lord," and believe in your heart that God raised him from the dead, you will be saved. For it is with your heart that you believe and are justified, and it is with your mouth that you confess and are saved.

As the Scripture says, "Anyone who trusts in him will never be put to shame. For the Lord is Lord of all and richly blesses all who call on him, for, "Everyone who calls on the name of the Lord will be saved."

Trail 1: List up to three shame-related actions (negative, harmful, self-destructive behaviors) you have committed *against yourself* during your life. Do this in point form and be brief. God already knows all the details.

Examples: denial, lying, reading or looking at pornography, masturbation, intentionally cutting yourself, suicide attempts, all addictive behavior patterns, all self-destructive behaviors, not letting others help you, etc.

	Action 1	Action 2	Action 3
Ages 0-10:			
Ages 11-15:			
Ages 16-20:			
Ages 21-25:			
Ages 26-35:			
Ages 35-present:			

Trail 2: List up to three shame-related actions (negative, harmful, and destructive behaviors) that were committed *by others against you **with your permission***.

Examples: Letting others make you do things you knew were wrong, harmful, shameful (you giving in to peer pressure, fear, needs).

	Action 1	Action 2	Action 3
Ages 0-10:			
Ages 11-15:			
Ages 16-20:			
Ages 21-25:			
Ages 26-35:			
Ages 35-present:			

Trail 3: List up to three shame-related actions (negative, harmful, and destructive behaviors) that were committed *by others against you **without your permission**.*

Examples: theft, acts of violence, rape, fraud, ID theft, gossip, false accusations, injustices, spouse/parent/family member/friend suicide, etc.

	Action 1	Action 2	Action 3
Ages 0-10:			
Ages 11-15:			
Ages 16-20:			
Ages 21-25:			
Ages 26-35:			
Ages 35-present:			

Trail 4: List up to three shame-related actions (negative, harmful, and destructive behaviors) that were committed *by you against others **with** their permission*.

Examples: Anytime you manipulated others to take advantage of them or convinced them it was okay to sin with or without your direct involvement.

	Action 1	Action 2	Action 3
Ages 0-10:			
Ages 11-15:			
Ages 16-20:			
Ages 21-25:			
Ages 26-35:			
Ages 35-present:			

Trail 5: List up to three shame-related actions (negative, harmful, and destructive behaviors) that were committed *by you against others **without** their permission*.

Examples: Here you are the offender, the one who victimizes, overriding other's wills and safety. These are acts of harm you did to others, because you wanted to or had to. Violence, stealing, sexual assault, murder, lying about them so they were injured, etc.

	Action 1	Action 2	Action 3
Ages 0-10:			
Ages 11-15:			
Ages 16-20:			
Ages 21-25:			
Ages 26-35:			
Ages 35-present:			

Lesson 9, Prayer Activity 4: Nailing Your Shame to the Cross

Nothing changes inside of you until you ask God to change it. When you go to God and ask Him to help you in Jesus' name, He responds because He loves you and because you are His child. You must be willing to name the things in your flesh that are causing you and others pain and let Him take them, believing (faith in Him) that He can and will heal you. God does this because of Jesus' sacrifice on the cross, not because you (we) deserve it. None of us deserves God's mercy. It is a free gift to us paid for with great pain by Jesus.

Some of the main sources of mental and relationship pain come from growing up in dysfunctional families. Listed below are a few of the things that can keep you trapped in the pain identified in the **Healing Your Five Trails of Shame** exercise. Pray to God about those you want Him to take from you, for example:

- The negative inner voice lies about my value to God.

- The negative impact of Dad's or Mom's behavior on my value of myself.

- The emotional pain I keep hanging on to which indicates I am not valuable.

- The shame I still feel for things I have done to myself and others.

- The shame and anger I feel for evil things done to me.

Father God, I have struggled with_____for many years, and it is causing me great pain. Please take it from me by washing my spirit clean from it. Please increase my faith in you Father, in the name of Jesus.

During the next week thank God each day for washing your mind clean even if your mind tells you the shame is still there or even if you feel like nothing has happened. This is your flesh trying to stay in control. Praise God ten times each morning, noon, and night for your healing. By your faith you shall be healed. If you need more faith, ask God for it.

Deep Healing: Section Three

Developing a Personal Protection
Plan in Jesus' Name

The Light of Scripture:

John 17:11, 15
I will remain in the world no longer, but they are still in the world, and I am coming to you. Holy Father, protect them by the power of your name-the name you gave me-so that they may be one as we are one.

My prayer is not that you take them out of the world but that you protect them from the evil one.

A Testimony to God's Deep Healing

I am very happy to share how God has gifted you to change people's life. It is extra special of course, because I was humbled to share it with Denise.

You will always hold a special place in my life, because of what Deep Healing has done for me. Also, the part you and Denise have brought to me, not only in the healing of my life but also growth through Our Lord. At the time in my life when I chose to take the Deep Healing class, I was struggling with many strongholds (or what some people would call baggage) in my life.

I had taken several Christian Bible classes, in addition to ongoing counseling, and still felt I was missing something deeper to release the deep root depression, sadness, sense of failure and my lack of value. Denise and Everett were my friends and had invited me to the Deep Healing class at our church. As God strongly nudged me, I felt it was time for me to take the next step.

What I have taken from the class has stayed with me from the moment I walked into the classroom. Everett taught me to stay "plugged in to God" every day and the importance of what that means. The structure of his workbook and how it leads you through healing the areas of your wounds, no matter how deep they are, can only be divine intervention. You receive the tools to work through those issues you are dealing with and understand why you have been experiencing what you feel, with biblical backup.

*Anyone who chooses to take the class, read and use the workbook will have their lives changes in ways that can only be done by the hand of God. May reading this give you the courage to take the next step in your life, to get the healing you desire through God.   **Michelle H.***

Deep Healing: Lesson Ten

The Skill of Protecting Your Life

A Testimony to God's Deep Healing

I have had many disappointments in my life. Praise the Lord; God has never been one of them. My story is 43 years in the making, but my life is just starting. I have always been defined by very intense mental lies and heavy-duty abandonment issues; just a body walking the earth with no sense of identity, feelings, or self-worth. Clearly I was alone, lost and had no chance of a fulfilling life. Then in May 2012 my world fell apart. I lost my daughter to her need to break away from my toxic, unhealthy, codependency, controlling ways. This put me over the edge. She was my everything, and without her, I had no purpose.

I was so alone and scared. I found myself returning to church, always sitting in the back—sneaking in and out, unknown. I began to ask God for direction and to help me heal and not feel so alone. I continued to pray for a healed heart and out of what I thought was the "blue" (it was really the Holy Spirit guiding me) I picked up the church winter class schedule and saw a class called Deep Healing by Denise and Everett.

I have been so blessed because of their obedience to let the Lord work through them. I have learned so much about myself, especially when I started "plugging in" to God. For the first time I began to feel loved, cherished, and worthy. Deep Healing has not always been comfortable to sit through—sometimes it was very scary and painful—but knowing that God is protecting me has made it all possible to go through.

Deep Healing has been so instrumental in teaching me basic truths and stepping-stones during my healing process. I believe the two most important things I will always remember are to plug in to God daily for my strength, and, that my flesh (negative inner voice) is not my friend. There is still so much work to be done on myself, but the Lord truly blessed me with the teaching in this book.

I pray that as you go on this new journey, God's direction for your life will be clear as you begin to recover and heal. I have been in this healing process of my heart for 11 months now. God has never abandoned me, always kept me protected and loved, and, for the first time in my life, I believe I am precious. I now look forward to living a life designed for a special purpose. I am a precious child of our God most high, and no matter what anyone has ever said about me, I am loved *and* worthy, *and so are* you!

Philippians 4:6-7
Don't worry about anything, instead pray about everything. Tell God what you need and thank him for all he has done. If you do this, you will experience God's peace, which is far more wonderful than the human mind can understand. His Peace will guard your hearts and minds as you live in Christ Jesus.

God bless and Praise the Lord,

Trish G.

Long, long time ago when there were large castles in small kingdoms, peasants (called serfs) lived outside the castle gates. As farm-workers they tended gardens, animals and large fields of crops for the land owner whom they called "Lord". The Lord owned the serfs as well as the land and they worked to provide him with the food they grew on his property. They also chopped wood from his trees and delivered it to the castle for heating and cooking, and they most likely spun wool from his sheep to provide clothes for their families. In return, the Lord let them keep part of the "fruits" from their labor and provided them with protection.

Inside the castle the Lord lived with his family, servants and soldiers. They obviously lived much better than the peasants. They had better shelter, plenty of food, better clothes, faster horses and everything else they needed to run the kingdom. The soldier's main purpose was to protect the kingdom which included the serfs. This was easy for them to do when everyone remained behind the strong, high walls of the castle and the draw bridge was raised.

When bandits or raiders did arrive in the kingdom, threatening to "kill, steal and destroy" whatever they could, most of the serfs would flee into the castle for security. Unfortunately, there were always some who wouldn't or couldn't make it in. The serfs that made it inside the walls were safe from the enemy. While those outside with the barbarians were considered "dead ducks".

When the kingdom was severely threatened by hostiles, several things made the difference between life and death. These key things were: the value of the walls, the effectiveness of the defense plan, the training of the soldiers, the obedience of the serfs, and the benevolence of the Lord. Let's examine each one as it relates to your healing:

1. Boundaries Built by God are your Castle Walls.

It makes sense that Castles back then needed high walls all the way around to keep barbarians out. If a castle had high walls in the front and short walls in the back, the hordes would simply go around to the weakest part of the wall and attack there.

It is the same thing when you require healing. You need boundaries that are strong enough to keep your invaders (greed, porn, alcohol, drugs, etc.) out. Your boundaries need to cover all of your life, not just certain parts of your Castle (life) leaving critical areas open for invasion. To do this you must gain self-control, which means control over your flesh, your sinful nature, and your body.

Proverbs 25:28
Like a city whose walls are broken down is a man who lacks self-control.

2. A Self-Protection Plan is required for a Successful Defense of Your Life

Defending Castles always required a plan of action. Everyone from the Lord, his knights and soldiers, right down to the serfs had jobs to do and do well, if they were to survive the attack. Each person went to their battle station and did what was required to survive the onslaught. Your restoration is no different. To protect your life, you must have a plan.

Having an effective plan is only half the battle. You must also execute the plan competently whenever it is needed. Any plan of defense that is ignored (or implemented slowly) quickly becomes useless. Plans that keep you safe are proactive, future focused, so that no one can sneak up on you. They also are designed to maximize your strengths and to eliminate your weaknesses before the barbarians are at the gate.

The enemy is relentless, strong and very shrewd. He does not just attack when you are expecting him. He is a 24-7 invader, looking for any advantage he can get to destroy you and your family. This is especially true when the enemy, more often than not, is the weaknesses in your own flesh. When your weaknesses connect with the world's temptations, you fall into wickedness. Even if it feels good, you are still sliding down into darkness without a way back out.

> **Mark 14:38**
> *Watch and pray so that you will not fall into temptation. The spirit is willing, but the body is weak.*

3. Your Personality and Body Parts are the Soldiers you must train to Stand Firm

Besides Castle walls protecting the serfs, there were also soldiers who had been trained to defend the Lord's property. They were well equipped and knew their opponents well enough to be ready at all times. In your recovery, these soldiers are those parts of your flesh that you control. Your will, mind, heart, feelings, needs, etc. all must be working with the plan rather than against it.

In history, many great battles and kingdoms were lost because of sabotage. When soldiers (who were trusted to fight for one side) suddenly turn and betrayed their side by providing crucial information that led to the enemy's success, sabotage occurred. As we have learned in previous lessons, our flesh is often sabotaging our recovery and health. You think your personality and body parts are on your side, but in reality they often are not, causing you to fail repeatedly in your attempt to gain freedom from compulsive, self-destructive behavior patterns.

You must learn to control yourself (flesh, body parts), if you are to win the fight. There is only one way you can succeed, and that is to teach (command) your flesh to Stand Firm under attack and to not give in to temptation. This requires you to be plugged into God's power and grace so you can stand firm against the adversary. Wearing God's armor always keeps you safe from the enemy's fiery arrows.

> **Ephesians 6:10-11**
> *Finally, be strong in the Lord and in his mighty power. Put on the full armor of God so that you can take your stand against the devil's schemes.*

4. Obedience to Your Lord's Will and Commands will save your Life

Timing is everything in an emergency. Minutes, even seconds, can make the difference from you being "almost harmed" or you going to the hospital, jail or ending up in the morgue. When the Lord calls you, come running and don't look back! Leave everything that hinders you getting behind safe walls. Hesitation has sent many a man into years of suffering, due to his wanting to stay outside the Lord's will just a little bit longer. When the Lord calls, run, don't stroll!

> **Proverbs 8:10**
> *The name of the Lord is a strong tower; the righteous run into it and are safe.*

So what keeps serfs (you) from coming into safety?

Many people want to obey God. They want to please him, but not just yet. They believe they can "have their cake and eat it too" which is an old saying meaning they want to keep living in sin and be blessed at the same time. God doesn't play that game. Here are a few reasons many people never make it back to safety:

A. Pride - thinking they can do whatever they want whenever they want.

B. Stupidity - they do not know the true danger of their choices and actions.

C. Too busy being self-indulgent to pay attention to obvious warning signs.

D. Do not want to leave their "stuff" (acting out) behind.

E. They have wandered too far away from the castle (Lord's will) to make it back on time.

F. Betraying the Lord and negotiating with the enemy to gain pleasure and payoffs.

G. Believing Satan's lie, "It will never happen to you!"

Healing Truth No. 51
Disobedience and self-abuse are never approved by God and therefore, can never be Healthy, Helpful or Holy.

5. The Lord's Mercy lets you inside the Kingdom

The best part of the Castle analogy is that the Lord values his serfs and wants all of them to come into safety. God wants you to receive His mercy and protection, but first you must let Him become Lord of your life. For me, it was the best gift I ever received in my life. I just regret taking so long to let it happen. One of the main reasons I rejected the gift for so long was that I did not value myself enough to protect myself. By not protecting myself, I let my body be abused by the sinful things I did outside of God's protection. I was stupid for not being afraid of my sin enough to run from it. When God says flee, He means run as fast as you can.

1 Corinthians 6:18-20
Flee from sexual immorality. All other sins a man commits are outside his body, but he who sins sexually sins against his own body. Do you not know that your body is a temple of the Holy Spirit, who is in you, whom you have received from God? You are not your own; you were bought at a price. Therefore honor God with your body.

Healing Truth No. 52
We don't protect what we don't value.

People with self-destructive behavior patterns do not realize or will not admit (denial) that they are destroying their bodies and lives. They need protection from themselves! To receive God's healing, you must be able to make the shift from not valuing yourself, to protecting yourself out of love. Many family members and friends just do not understand why we do not just stop doing whatever it is that is destroying our world. The answer is, "We don't protect what we don't value!"

As we learned in the Self-Worth lesson, individuals with low self-worth place little if any value on whom they are. Their very strong negative inner voices keep telling them they are losers, worthless, incompetent and will never accomplish anything so why would they "think" they are valuable enough to protect, to fight for? If the negative inner voice is not transformed into a loving, positive inner voice, then no individual can learn how to protect themselves. No boundaries (walls of safety) will ever work, because they refuse to enforce them.

Here's a simple example; let's say I own a nice house that is not very old and I have a very expensive alarm system in it. If I never turn it on when I leave, it would indicate that I don't value anything in the house enough to protect it. In short, I don't care if someone comes and destroys it. Your body is the "nice house" God has given you to live in while here on earth. If you are not protecting it then you have low self-worth, a negative inner voice, and are so nonassertive (passive or aggressive) that you will not fight to protect yourself and those you love.

As you read in Lesson 8, low self-esteem means you are not a friend to yourself. You do not like who you are and hate being alone. You have no love for yourself, so you let yourself be abused and continue to put your body in harmful situations and relationships. Yet, if your best friend came to you for help you would treat them better than you treat yourself, because you value them (their house) more. Do you help them or tell them they deserve to suffer? I would hope that you would care for them.

So, why should it be any different when you turn to yourself for caring and help? Many times others are not available and you need to help yourself immediately. You need to learn to treat yourself as you would treat your best friend, if they came to you with the problem. See yourself as valuable as Jesus sees you. Holding yourself accountable for your healing is love not hate.

So What is Love?

I know I have already used this verse previously in the book, but it is exactly the one that fits here:

> **1 Corinthians 13:4-7**
> *Love is patient, love is kind. It does not envy, it does not boast, it is not proud. It is not rude, it is not self-seeking, it is not easily angered, it keeps no record of wrongs. Love does not delight in evil but rejoices with the truth. It always protects, always trusts, always hopes, always perseveres.*

As I started my inner healing, God brought me to this verse often and it was very hard to admit that I was just the opposite, especially towards me. I wasn't patient or kind. I was envious, boastful and prideful. I was rude, self-absorbed, and had a bad temper with a long memory of those who had harmed me. I found way too much pleasure in worldly things and very little in learning.

Yet, as I started to trust God with my healing, I found that the truth Jesus speaks in His word was protecting me. It was giving me hope and strength to keep going when I wanted to quit, which was almost daily. God's love for me slowly changed me back into the person He created me to be, and with His love I started to love myself as well as others.

Your healing needs fuel to drive it through all the mud and tough roads you have to travel. This fuel is Love. As you let God fill up your tank, you will find amazing power to get up and get it done. You will feel successful over areas of your life that you long thought would never be conquered. You will have hope that your future life will not be a repeat of your past life. You will also become assertive ("Stand Firm") in front of the enemy; you will not run away, give-in or give up, and you will not let your flesh help the enemy to destroy your life.

Assertiveness is the Skill of Protecting the Helpless and Yourself

I find that many people do not understand what assertiveness is because they cannot identify what the behavior actually looks like. It can be very confusing because it is a "multifaceted" skill that consists of many other skills. It also can be difficult to comprehend because it depends on many different social circumstances. For instance, displaying a certain behavior pattern in one social situation might be considered aggressive and in another it is considered assertive. So, how can you know what it is and how to develop it to protect the helpless and yourself?

Let's begin by helping you understand what it "looks like" when comparing it to two other, more commonly known interpersonal style categories: passive and aggressive. The key concepts that separate these three interpersonal styles of behavior are outlined in the
Understanding Assertiveness Chart.

Understanding Assertiveness Chart

	Aggressive	Passive	Assertive
Relationship Attitude & Approach	Win-Lose Thinker Competitive	Lose-Win Thinker Unhappy Servant	Win-Win Thinker Teammate, Partner
Proactive-Reactive Thinking	Externally Reactive, "Greedy" thinkers	Internally Reactive, "Fearful" thinkers	Internally/Externally Proactive, "Optimistic" thinkers
Self-Worth Level	Low	Low	High
Protection Focus	Self only, harms others	None	Self and the helpless
Rights	Want theirs and yours	Believe they have none	Believe people have God-given rights
Responsibilities	Refuse them, reject	Feel obligated for theirs and yours	Accept responsibility for their behavior only
Emotional Triggers	Anger, jealousy, losing anything	Fear, pain, hurt	Injustice, dishonesty
Situational Triggers	People telling them no, having their aggressiveness challenged	Conflict, threats, demands made upon them, being yelled at, seeing others suffer	Innocent being hurt, criminal behavior, the helpless being taken advantage of
Boundaries	Boundary busters	No Boundaries	Boundary setters
Roles played	Takers, Dominators, Controllers, Blamers, Bullies, Abusers	Marks, Floor mats, Victims, Martyrs, Nurses,	Protectors, Providers Planners, Leaders, Problem solvers

Aggressive people want all their rights and yours as well, which is why they are perceived as "takers". They "fake people out" by acting secure but underneath all their bluster they really are very insecure and have low self-worth. They are competitive in all that they do believing that they either win or they will lose. This leads them to become controllers.

Aggressive people also do not accept responsibility for their errors in life and blame their mistakes on others. They are fear driven and are very reactive to worldly pressures. They operate by using intimidation to scare others (passives) into giving them what they want. They are often perceived as: abusers, bullies, villains, dominators, criminals and selfish.

Passive people have low self-worth. They don't believe they are worthy of any rights. To feel useful and to keep relationships at home and at work secure, they take on others responsibilities as well as their own. They are perceived as martyrs, targets and "floor mats" by aggressive people. Passive people live under a heavy stress load, as they let aggressive people walk all over them. It doesn't take too much thinking to figure out that aggressive people "mark" passive people for abuse. The passive person gives in, because they hate "conflict" and believe (negative inner voice lie) that if they give the aggressor what they want they will stop hurting them. It actually works the opposite way, once the aggressive person gets something they always come back for more.

Assertive people take responsibility for what they are responsible for and nothing else. They stand up for their rights and refuse to take rights away from others. This style does not match the aggressive person who gets very frustrated (angry) when they meet assertive people who will not give in to their demands. Assertive people are way too much work and too big a threat to aggressive people, so they try to stay away from them. Passive (marks) people are much easier to use and abuse.

A key difference between assertive people and the other two types of interpersonal styles is assertive people will do what it takes to protect themselves because they have high self-worth. They value their lives enough to protect themselves from anything (including their own flesh) that would destroy them. This means removing themselves from danger, not just fighting it.

Assertiveness can be described as "the skill of protecting yourself" from you, others and from the world. For instance, if you repeatedly put yourself in dangerous situations that can bring extreme harm to your body and to your life you are not being assertive. As we have read previously your body is the temple of the Holy Spirit and God takes exception to any negative treatment of it.

Healing Truth No. 53
The success of your healing all depends upon how solid your spiritual foundation is.

The world of architecture and its achievements has always amazed me. A basic building principle in creating any architectural structure is that the foundation or base must be much broader (larger) than the rest of the structure if it is going to be able to carry the load or weight for a long period of time. The bridge, arch and pyramid are all prime examples of this principle. In recovery finding forgiveness, healing, and restoration all require a large base from which to build upon if your recovery is to last the test of time. You must learn how to "Stand Firm" in God's power and to do this you must have faith.

> **Romans 10:17**
> *Consequently, faith comes from hearing the message, and the message is heard through the word of Christ.*

The following **Stand Firm (Spiritual Assertiveness) Pyramid** illustrates this principle and also identifies other qualities and skills needed to be assertive.

The Assertiveness Pyramid

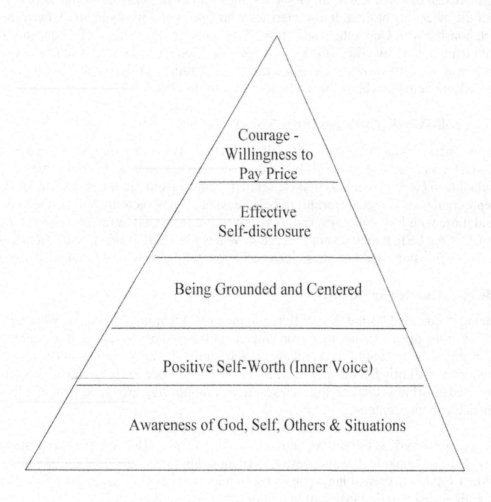

Courage -
Willingness to
Pay Price

Effective
Self-disclosure

Being Grounded and Centered

Positive Self-Worth (Inner Voice)

Awareness of God, Self, Others & Situations

Healing Truth No. 54
Healthy change requires learning how to replace negative habits with healthy behaviors.
Learning who God is through His Holy Word must happen first for this to bring healing.

Let's review each section starting with the foundation of the pyramid.

1. Awareness of God's Truth vs. Self, Others, Things and Time

Knowledge needs to start with God (His truths) and work down towards earth and humans, not the other way around. It also clarifies who God is and who you are. It defines your relationship with God, others and "things". It provides answers to life's questions and helps you learn how to live life. This knowledge from God's word comes from the Holy Spirit as you read and memorize it. Increased awareness (truth) clarifies what is from God and what is evil and helps you know how valuable you are to God.

2. High Self-Worth (Christian Inner Voice)

You cannot change if your mind is full of lies that say you are useless and can never be saved (reconciled and changed) by God. You need to accept and believe that you are highly valuable to God, so much so that He sent His Son Jesus to die for you. Then let God reprogram your computer (brain) to believe what He says is truth. To change you need love, and those with low self-worth cannot receive love from God or anyone else because they are stuck in the lie that they do not deserve it. When you value yourself and others as God values you, your mind becomes clearer and you will become more grounded and centered.

3. Being Grounded and Centered

Being "Grounded" is the skill of living in the now. Learning to focus on what you need to be doing in the present rather than worrying about the past or the future. Jesus talks about focusing only on "today" in Matthew 6:34, because you have no guarantees of what tomorrow will bring. You only learn in the "now" (the present), when you are completely focused on what you are trying to learn. If you cannot stay grounded, you will have great difficulty being centered.

Being "Centered" is the skill of "knowing who you are". This involves understanding what you believe, think, feel, value, desire, need, and what your strengths and weaknesses are. When you know these things, you can surrender them to God easier than if you do not know that they are operating inside of you in negative, ungodly ways.
When you are centered, you know what your "identity" really is. You know who God created you to be rather than who the world says you should be. Memorizing God's word (bible verses) grounds and centers you in the truth, exposing lies (evil) for what they really are; messages from Satan.

People who are not grounded and centered have great difficulty self-disclosing in healthy ways. They often are "not sure" of who they are or what they are responsible for. Denial is a key indicator of people who struggle with these two skills. Often when you ask them direct questions about their internal experiences they answer, "I don't know" or tell you something someone else says about them, because they do not know. In this condition, they are easily misled into darkness.

4. **Healthy Self-disclosure/Transparency**

Healthy self-disclosure can only occur if you are being controlled by the Holy Spirit because only God knows what is healthy and what is not. His words in Scripture help you understand the difference between being righteous and sinful. To be healed you must take responsibility for your mistakes and character flaws. You must be able to articulate internal things within your personality that are harming you and misleading you into sinful behaviors, relationships and situations. This skill is called "transparency" and requires individuals to tell the truth so they are "transparent" before God and appropriate others.

Transparency is being honest about yourself with others in an appropriate manner. Appropriate means sharing "in the right way, to the right person, at the right time". This usually occurs with your accountability partner or in a support group or with a professional helper. It does not mean you go and tell your "story" to anyone and everyone such as family members, co-workers or neighbors…all who may mean well but lack the helping knowledge you require. And once you share to the wrong person, it is out there and it is impossible to get it back. So using Social Media sites to be transparent can be very risky. Think twice before you hit the send button

5. **Courage/Willingness to pay the Price**

Standing Firm (being assertive) takes great courage. It is hard to stand for righteousness when the majority around you wants to be immoral. It is very unpopular and as Jesus has warned us in Matthew 10:22 "All men will hate you because of me" and John 3:20, "Everyone who does evil hates the light." You have to be willing to pay the price, like Paul and Silas did in Acts, when they preached the truth about Jesus. Sadly, I have worked with many men in recovery who could not (would not) quit their acting out, because they cared more about what people (friends, family) said than what Jesus said.

1 Timothy 4:13
Until I come, devote yourself to the public reading of Scripture, to preaching and to teaching.

Healing Truth No. 55
You are commanded to dedicate yourself to preaching and teaching God's truth but you can't teach what you haven't learned.

Giving testimony about what God has done in your life, preaching His Holy Word to the lost and teaching God's truths to the spiritually immature all require the skill of assertiveness. They all require you to Stand Firm upon the rock (Jesus). True believers are commanded to do this in the power of the Holy Spirit until Jesus comes again.

Lesson 10, Prayer Activity 1: How successfully do you Stand Firm?

Stand Firm/Assertiveness Characteristics	I Seldom do this	I do this about half the time	I do this over 80% of the time
Communicate your beliefs, needs & feelings clearly			
Refuse to let bitterness/ anger ruin your relationships			
Refuse to accept or defend others non-assertive attitudes and behavior			
Take full responsibility for your speech, behavior			
Are loving, kind, respectful towards self and others			
Protect yourself financially, handle money wisely			
Protect yourself mentally, emotionally, physically and spiritually			
Ask God and others for help when you need it			
Apologize when you make mistakes or are wrong			
Reward self for your effort as well as for success			
Let God turn your negatives into positives			
Surround yourself with believers who are positive			
Set and protect boundaries in all areas of your life			
Respect other's assertive behavior, boundaries			
Live by Faith in God not fear of man, situations			
Forgive others whether they ask for it or not			
Say yes when you mean yes and no when it is no			
Keep your promises and commitments, if possible			
Fellowship with believers, friends and family			
Stand Firm against manipulation, demands, threats			
Call for help before you fall into temptation, sin			
Play, laugh and enjoy life as well as work hard			
Proactively live following your protection plan			

Lesson 10, Prayer Activity 2: Nailing Your "Non-assertiveness" to the Cross

Nothing changes inside of you until you ask God to change it. When you go to God and ask Him to help you in Jesus' name He responds because He loves you and because you are His child. You must be willing to name the things in your flesh that are causing you and others pain and let Him take them believing (faith in Him) that He can and will heal you. God does this because of Jesus' sacrifice on the cross not because you (we) deserve it. None of us deserves God's mercy. It is a free gift to us paid for with great pain by Jesus.

Some of the main sources of mental and relationship pain come from growing up in dysfunctional families. Listed below are a few of the things that can keep you trapped in the pain identified in the "We Don't Protect What We Don't Value" lesson. Pray to God for those you want him to take from you, for example:

- Lack of value you have placed on yourself

- Passive behavior patterns that harm you and others

- Aggressive behavior patterns that harm you and others

- Fear that runs and ruins your life

- Laziness that keeps you from learning how to be assertive

- Lack of courage to Stand Firm

- Disobedience regarding Jesus commands to tell others about Him

Father God, I have struggled with_____ for many years, and it is causing me great pain. Please take it from me by washing my spirit clean from it. Please increase my faith in you, in the name of Jesus.

During the next week thank God every day for "washing your mind clean" even if your mind tells you it is still there or you feel like nothing has happened. This is your flesh trying to stay in control. Praise God ten times morning, noon and night for your healing. By your Faith you shall be healed. If you need more faith, ask God for it.

Deep Healing: Lesson Eleven

Living in Bounds

The Light of Scripture:

1 Peter 1:13-14
Therefore, prepare your minds for action; be self-controlled; set your hope fully on the grace to be given you when Jesus Christ is revealed. As obedient children, do not conform to the evil desires you had when you lived in ignorance.

A Testimony to God's Deep Healing

Whoa! This is an amazing book for ANYONE and everyone. As a woman, I found it extremely valuable as it revealed to me just how dangerous my flesh really can be. This book showed me in a personal way how to receive permanent healing and victory.

No one book I have read has dealt with the deep personal needs we all have like the writer does in this book. It is also, in part, a personal workbook which makes the truth hit home faster. The author is obviously a strong servant of the Lord and uses Scripture throughout the book. Having read this book, I now know I can win the war with my flesh!

The many activities in this book will help those struggling with how to find help. The greatest concept I found is that "our flesh is not our friend" which is explained completely and with humor throughout the book. By sharing his personal struggles throughout the lessons, it helps the reader easily relate to his teaching.

The teaching is at a deep level yet it is presented as simple and easy to comprehend. If you are seeking freedom from any pain, sadness or addiction, I urge you to read this book. The lesson on setting boundaries alone is worth the price of the book.

Paulette B.

One of the saddest counseling sessions I ever had was with a young man who came to me because he was depressed. As I listened to his story I started to feel depressed too. His Father taught him how to ski and together they skied often in the mountains above Vancouver, British Columbia. Some of his greatest memories with his father came from skiing together.

However, the last time they skied together his dad challenged him to race down the mountain to see who would come in first. He had never beaten his dad but he was now big enough and strong enough to do it, so he eagerly accepted the challenge. As they flew down the slope at top speed he could see his dad out of the corner of his eyes but then he was gone. Figuring he was behind him he pushed harder and made it down to the bottom of the run. When he stopped and looked back up the hill he couldn't see his dad.

He waited for about ten minutes and then realized something must have happened. He went up the hill calling for his dad but there was no answer. After searching, he skied down to the aid station and asked for help. Immediately rescue skiers arrived and the search continued. Sadly, they found his dad face down in a deep hole full of snow which suffocated him.

What made this story so tragic is that his dad always taught him to never ski out of bounds but on this particular day his dad did just that. Trying to beat his son down the hill to win the contest dad took a "short-cut" that looked so inviting with perfect snow and no observable hazards. But hitting an unseen hazard underneath the snow flipped him over causing him to land head first into a very deep drift. He could not get out by himself and no one was there to help him.

The only comfort from this sad experience was that the son ended up being a ski instructor who taught young skiers to never ski out of bounds, but he did so in a unique way. By sharing his grief he helped them understand the importance of obeying safety rules and not risking the danger of skiing out of bounds. He helped them to understand that breaking boundaries always brings unfortunate consequences.

Breaking boundaries can happen in a moment or it can occur over a long period of time. Are you pushing your boundaries, testing them to see if you are stronger than what they are protecting you from? Do you currently have boundaries? Do you really understand what they are? Are you "skiing within" your boundaries? Or are you taking high risks by crossing over to what appears on the surface to be safe but is really destruction waiting to claim you? Are you causing overwhelming pain to yourself and those who love you?

This lesson will help you to understand that setting boundaries requires you to say "no" to your flesh and "yes" to God. To do this requires the ability to control self (flesh) so it is not controlling you. Boundaries are only functional and valuable if you are assertive and stand firm against your flesh, the world and Satan.

Titus 2:11-12
For the grace of God that brings salvation has appeared to all men. It teaches us to say "No" to ungodliness and worldly passions and to live self-controlled, upright and godly lives in this present age...

Healing Truth No. 56
A boundary is anything that protects you from a harmful person, event or situation. To be a boundary, it must protect you from: 1. your flesh, 2. the world, and 3. Satan.

Setting Boundaries protects others as well as yourself.

Traditionally, a boundary was a mark that divides something into two. Every nation has boundaries, what are often called borders, indicating where each nation begins and ends. These markers let people know when they are in one country or another. Boundaries are only functional and valuable if they clearly indicate when you are inside or outside of a boundary.

There are many other kinds of boundaries besides physical ones. In Exodus 20 God gave Moses the Ten Commandments which are moral boundaries for us to follow if we want to please God. Moral boundaries are often referred to as, "Dos and Don'ts". The Ten Commandments were specifically designed to keep you safe. When you go outside of them you put yourself and others in harm's way. God gave you these limitations to protect you from the consequences which lie outside of His rules (His will) for healthy living.

A boundary provides a buffer with enough personal space for you to maneuver away from harm and back to safety. For example, my house provides me with a safe place to rest, rejoice and relax from every day pressures that are stressful. It also gives me protection from bad weather, extreme heat or cold, and from people who want to take what I own. My protection from its boundaries disappears as soon as I go outside my house.

For more of an in-depth understanding of your protection plan think of boundaries in each of the following three things:

1. **Protection Plans**
   Unfortunately, to survive and succeed in life you need many boundaries, not just one. Each boundary acts like a protection plan that helps you to avoid being overwhelmed by negative situations and stimulates you to thrive in positive ones.

2. **Protection Tools**
   Boundaries are protective devices or tools that keep you safe. They are similar to brakes, lights, seatbelts and airbags in your automobile. Most of the time you don't overly focus on these things yet once a serious accident takes plac, you are glad they are there.
   While these safety devices may not completely protect you in an auto accident you are much better off with them than without them. So it is with your personal boundaries.

3. **A Protective Force Field**
   Lastly, visualize boundaries as force fields that surround you with a layer of defenses from which you can make healthy decisions. If you have a solid plan and the tools necessary you can create a field or zone of protection. To keep any force field or boundary functional it requires power, maintenance and plan revision. Therefore, the main threat to your boundaries is You. You need to keep God's power coming into the boundary to keep it in place. You need to maintain your boundaries to be sure they fit the threats you need to stand firm against, and lastly you need to revise your boundaries as needed.

If you lack energy (power) you cannot have boundaries. No energy, no shield - no shield, no protection. God's Holy Spirit provides that energy if you surrender your will to Him daily and ask for His grace to protect you.

In life there are many areas that need boundaries.

Your cravings, compulsions and habitual ways of responding all point to areas that need removal. It is your responsibility to make sure you do not let your sinful nature connect to the evil in the world. That connection will only lead to a loss of safety for you and your family. That connection will lead you to ski out of bounds and into danger and pain every time.

And this presents a very big challenge as there are so many life areas that require boundaries.

Here are just a few examples:

- Your Body - what you do with your body parts (hands, arms, legs, feet, brain, etc.)
- Honesty- frequency for telling the truth, not stealing or deceiving
- Emotional Distance - intimacy and closeness vs. isolation & depression
- Geographical Distance - how close you let toxic people get to you
- Time - who controls this in your life, you or something or someone else?
- Relationships – choosing healthy vs. toxic interactions with people
- Consequences - taking ownership for your mistakes vs. blaming others
- Your Finances – how you use money unwisely, protection from debt
- Your Thinking – not letting your mind think of (focus on) sinful thoughts

Healing Truth No. 57
Healing is all about "living here" (inside God's protection) and "not there" (outside of God's protection).

There are two types of boundaries you will need to create to be effective.

There are two main kinds of boundaries or areas where you need protection from something or someone who will harm you. These two areas are defined by internal and external threats. You need to set boundaries for each area. If you do not have internal boundaries, you cannot maintain external boundaries. And if you do not have external boundaries, you will not be able to retain your internal boundaries.

A. Internal Boundaries (you stopping pollution from your flesh hurting you or others)

In the previous lessons I have identified many things inside of your personality and flesh that require strong management. Each one can lead you into self-destructive behavior patterns if you let them control you. In fact, self-control is self-management. Your will, for instance, is very strong and can mislead you if you don't have a way of controlling it. Feelings and emotions are other "things" inside of us that get us into trouble all the time. It is good to have them but you must not let them control your decisions and behavior.

Other internal areas that require boundaries are the left and right brain. You must have power and a plan that keeps your inner voice positive and the theatre of the mind playing healthy "movies" and images. Screening unhealthy thoughts and images from entering your brain in the first place creates a very solid boundary. If you teach "right and wrong" and "dos and don'ts to your children for their safety you must first protect the source of that teaching which is your mind.

And the internal list goes on and on: pride, fear, greed, desires, gluttony, hatred, bitterness, lust, criticalness, slander, and dishonesty to name a few.

B. External Boundaries (you stopping worldly pollution from Satan coming into you)

Anything outside of your skin and your behavior (actions) that threatens to hurt you falls into the external boundary area. The friend you spend time with who always has the extra "smoke" or "drink" you don't need. Maybe the work environment that abuses you mentally and emotionally creating high levels of stress in you. That special restaurant or drive-by fast food joint that serves up the "high-cal" diet that is slowly killing you. The porn shop you sometimes visit on the way home from work every day that feeds garbage into your mind.

James 1:27
Religion that God our Father accepts as pure and faultless is this: to look after orphans and widows in their distress and to keep oneself from being polluted by the world.

I think you get my point on this one. There are lots and lots of things and places in the world you must avoid and not partake of if you are to stay healthy (unpolluted). To do this you need a plan that not only keeps you from these things but one that also rewards you for doing so. The results can be devastating if you fail to set internal and external boundaries. I believe this section of Luke clearly speaks to the consequences of failing to plan:

Luke 8:11-15
This is the meaning of the parable: The seed is the word of God. Those along the path are the ones who hear, and then the devil comes and takes away the word from their hearts, so that they cannot believe and be saved. (These people have no internal or external boundaries)

Those among the rock are the ones who receive the word with joy when they hear it, but they have no root. They believe for a while, but in time of testing they fall away. (These people have no internal or external boundaries)

The seed that fell among thorns stands for those who hear, but as they go on their way they are choked by life's worries, riches and pleasures, and they do not mature.
(These people have no internal or external boundaries)

But the seed on good soil stands for those with a noble and good heart, who hear the word, retain it, and by persevering produce a crop.
(These people have both internal and external boundaries)

Healing Truth No. 58
Creating Boundaries is where the tires of recovery turn onto the road of healing.

I have known many people who have spent years in recovery but have never experienced healing. To recover your sanity and health you need to stop the force and direction of your negative actions and turn your life around by driving it back in the opposite direction. The "Assassins" (your flesh, the World and Satan) fully intend to destroy you when you try to turn your life around. If you do not put a protective force between you and them they will do so. Only when you are plugged in to God can you put a protective barrier between you and something that is a threat to your safety. So how is that actually done?

Every Healing Target (HT) Requires a Boundary.

Establishing internal boundaries requires that you identify those things you are currently doing to hurt others and yourself. These things become your Healing Targets (HTs). Internal HTs include the secrets you don't want others to know about you. It is your shame list. Jesus said that the "Truth will set you free!" By creating a complete list of your destructive behavior patterns and sharing with a few trustworthy people you can begin the process of being held accountable. This process is only helpful if you then eliminate those preferences, patterns, and rituals. You can do this by creating boundaries for each one following the action plan below.

Each HT consists of a series of negative behavioral steps that take you to the target. When you identify those steps and put boundaries at each step the action plan protects you from making it to the Target which is the purpose of having boundaries. You need to identify the steps that will help you to achieve your HT; this includes a weekly frequency count of how many times you broke your boundary by not taking your healing steps. Writing your score down will give you a visual aid to help you see where you need more work to achieve your healing target.

Example:

Internal Target	**Steps leading to Unhealthy Behavior**
Stop hating my father when I think of him	1. Dwelling on how dad harmed me
	2. I become overly emotional (sad, mad, etc.)
	3. I let emotions influence me to make bad decisions, do bad things
	4. I hate myself because I did something stupid/sinful again

Simply stopping destructive behavior is not enough. For boundaries to be effective, you must also **replace** all destructive behaviors (HTs) with healthy goals (HG). Every healthy goal has a series of action steps you must consistently do for them to become a healthy "habit". Let's take a look at a series of behaviors that can help you stop the negative series of behaviors listed above. When the first negative step comes up, you should immediately replace it with the positive first step.

Recovery Goal:	**Steps Stopping the Acting Out**
Forgive father	1. Pray to Jesus and ask for strength (plugging-in)
	2. Recite one bible verse that brings me strength everyday
	3. Call a support person <u>before</u> I act out and ask for prayer
	4. Write a letter to father, identifying the things he did wrong to me and then forgive him in Jesus' name (<u>Do not</u> reread or mail the letter when done, burn it.)

Healing Truth No. 59
Those who plan to work, work the plan. Those who fail to plan, plan to fail.

The main strategy in a healing plan is to replace every unhealthy behavior pattern with a **much stronger healthy behavior pattern**. Basically, you want to "Blow up the pathway to every source of pain" by creating a new pathway to utilizing God's power. If the new, healthy behavior pattern is not powered by God it will leave you weak and unsatisfied, and you will return (relapse) to your previous self-destructive patterns.

To build boundaries that work requires knowing and applying everything you have learned up to this lesson. Making a healing plan is hard work and maintaining it can be difficult. The activities in this workbook will help you create one that is tailored to your situation. Take the time to complete them and you will find out just how helpful a healing plan is to staying healthy. Everyday the choice is yours. I pray to choose to let God keep you Standing Firm (assertive) in His power.

Healing Truth No. 60
Boundaries without the power of the Holy Spirit may help you a little in this life, but they won't help you enter the Kingdom of God at all.

> **John 3:5**
> *I tell you the truth, unless a man is born of water and the Spirit, he cannot enter the kingdom of God. Flesh gives birth to flesh, but the Spirit gives birth to spirit. You must not be surprised at my saying, "You must be born again."*

Lesson 11, Prayer Activity 1: Are you Ready and Willing?

This means: are you ready and willing to share the plan with a recovery partner who will hold you accountable in love? Check the level you are currently at for each Recovery Plan prerequisite/goal:

A. Readiness Check: **Don't Do   Do 50/50   Do Daily**

1. Surrender your will and the battle with your flesh to God daily.   _____   _____   _____

2. Confess Your Sins – Keep short accounts, confess to God quickly.   _____   _____   _____

3. Convert Your Lifestyle – Renew your mind, heart, values, change your behavior.   _____   _____   _____

4. Commit to God's Purpose (not yours) for your Life. Set new goals to serve others.   _____   _____   _____

5. Eliminate Isolation and your "Secret" Life (all acting out).   _____   _____   _____

6. Identify clear "Boundaries" that protect you and others.   _____   _____   _____

7. Create a Support Network. Work only with those who build you up both spiritually and emotionally.   _____   _____   _____

8. Plan to work and work the Plan on a hourly, daily, weekly basis. Recovery takes time.   _____   _____   _____

9. Have mercy on yourself as Jesus has mercy on you.   _____   _____   _____

10. Praise God for everything, His discipline as well as His mercies and blessings.   _____   _____   _____

Circle the steps you marked "Don't Do" and "50/50". You must complete these on a daily basis to have a plan that will lead you out of insanity and into sobriety.

B. Willingness Check: Mark below how willing you are to recover from darkness.

Not Very Willing ....Sort of Willing.........................Totally Willing

Anything less than total willingness will sabotage your recovery plan.

Lesson 11, Prayer Activity 2: Targeting Threats to You and Others

A. Identify Healing Plan Targets

A healing target is anything that needs a boundary put between it and you to protect you and others. Healing targets are often the "demands and commands" on your life. Healing targets are anything that lead you into pain; anything that breaks your promise, commitment and focus on God. For instance, a financial healing target could be you misusing your credit card to sin.

Target Categories (circle the ones you need to create boundaries for):

- Emotions (yours or others) – anger, fear, loneliness, sadness, grief, impulsiveness, bitterness, envy, hate, depression, feeling unvalued.

- Family – Any reaction to (or by) a family member that sets you up to behave negatively – criticalness, rejection, domination, disrespect, dishonesty.

- Financial – A spending "habit" that pays for self-destructive behavior or creates debt stress that drives you into other ineffective behavior patterns – gambling, shopaholic, misusing credit cards, eating out too much.

- Internet – Wasting time reading worldly news that is all about murders, going to XXX web sites, toxic chat rooms, internet sex lines, compulsive online shopping, gambling, emailing or face booking with those who are bringing you down.

- Home – Things at home that cause you to sin – bad movies, music, alcohol, computers, unhealthy drugs, unhealthy foods, excessive TV, etc.

- Mental – Thoughts that set you up to fail – sexual thoughts, coveting "things" others have, judgmentalness, fantasies, worries, fears, revenge.

- Neighborhood – Anything in a one-mile radius of your house that you need to stay away from – stores, people, places, situations, etc.

- People – Anyone who leads you into sinful thinking and/or behavior – bosses, co-workers, co-students, family members, neighbors, strangers.

- Phone – Using your phone to talk or text dishonest, depraved things.

- Physical – Unhealthy things you need to stop doing with your body parts – talking, touching, walking/driving to places where you should not go.

B. Prioritize Healing Target Categories (rank the most serious ones first)

1.
2.
3.
4.
5.
6.
7.
8.
9.

C. Set Boundaries (turning negatives into positives)

Definitions:

Target	– Behavior you want to stop
Goal	– Behavior you want to start
Boundary	– What you **promise** God you will do to change targets into goals.

Examples:

Target (STOP)	Goal (START)	Boundary (protection from evil) (Your commitment, promise, request to God for protection)
1. Using Credit Cards to Sin	Use cards as God wills	1. Pray over cards, ask God to wash you clean of overspending and being a "shopaholic" 2. Share your Boundary Plan with your accountability partner 3. Lock cards up where you cannot get to them 4. Show all credit card statements to an accountability partner
2. Stop wasting Time watching TV, computer	Read God's word instead	1. Pray for power to cancel cable/satellite TV 2. Call and cancel cable/satellite TV 3. Read 1 Chapter in the bible one hour before bed 4. Record name and number of bible chapter daily on a calendar

Lesson 11, Prayer Activity 3: Boundaries Protect You from Habits and Rituals

Freedom comes when you replace unhealthy behavior patterns with healthy ones. This occurs when you target behavior patterns (habits, rituals) that keep taking you into painful (sinful) situations. A "**Habit**" is a series of behavior steps you take on a regular basis. It is your "pattern" for reaching the high (medication) you are seeking. A "**Ritual**" is a habit that controls you totally. After reviewing the example below list four Habits and Rituals that you want to change.

1. EXAMPLE	Steps that keep "it" happening (behaviors to stop doing)	Steps that make "it" change (behaviors to start doing)
Buying/renting bad movies	1. Theater of the mind shows "bad" images and you watch	1. Get on knees & pray, Praise God for 10 things
	2. Get money to buy or rent movies	2. Give all money, credit cards and check book to someone else
	3. Drive by video store	3. Drive to a friend's house or have a friend over instead
	4. Go in and get movie, go home and watch it	4. Read all of John in the bible, talking to Jesus as you do

The easiest step to win the battle is on step one, then two, then three. It is very hard to succeed if you wait until step four, by then you are committed to do the acting out and your flesh is controlling you. Have a plan in place and follow the plan before getting to steps three and four.

1. Recovery Target	Steps that keep it happening (behaviors to stop doing)	Steps that make it change (behaviors to start doing)
	1.	1.
	2.	2.
	3.	3.
	4.	4.

2. Recovery Target	Steps that keep it happening (behaviors to stop doing)	Steps that make it change (behaviors to start doing)
	1.	1.
	2.	2.
	3.	3.
	4.	4.

3. Recovery Target

<u>Steps that keep it happening</u> (behaviors to stop doing)	<u>Steps that make it change</u> (behaviors to start doing)
1.	1.
2.	2.
3.	3.
4.	4.

4. Recovery Target

<u>Steps that keep it happening</u> (behaviors to stop doing)	<u>Steps that make it change</u> (behaviors to start doing)
1.	1.
2.	2.
3.	3.
4.	4.

5. Recovery Target

<u>Steps that keep it happening</u> (behaviors to stop doing)	<u>Steps that make it change</u> (behaviors to start doing)
1.	1.
2.	2.
3.	3.
4.	4.

Habits and Rituals will bring you short-term pleasure and long-term pain. Boundaries, on the other hand, bring you short term pain and long term (eternal) gain.

Lesson 11, Prayer Activity 4: How to Set Internal/External Boundaries Establishing boundaries for your recovery should always be divided into Internal and External threat categories, each with at least one recovery target. Identify the threats you are targeting on the left side and then list the behavioral steps that you need to stop and start to get healthier.

A. Internal Threats	Current Recovery Targets (behavior to stop doing)	Protection Plan/Steps (behavior to start doing)
Boundaries that Protect You from:		
A. Your "Negative Self-Talk" (Left brain)	1. 2. 3. 4.	1. 2. 3. 4.
B. Your unhealthy Fantasies (Right brain)	1. 2. 3. 4.	1. 2. 3. 4.
C. Your Needs (i.e., respect, security, independence, safety, acceptance, etc.) Strongest Need	1. 2. 3. 4.	1. 2. 3. 4.
D. Your Wants (i.e., new car, electronics, clothes, house, promotion, etc.) Strongest Want	1. 2. 3. 4.	1. 2. 3. 4.
E. Your Fears (i.e., rejection, violence, failure, being unloved, etc.) Strongest Fear	1. 2. 3. 4.	1. 2. 3. 4.
F. Your Emotions (i.e., anger, loneliness, bitterness, unforgiveness, etc.) Strongest Emotion	1. 2. 3. 4.	1. 2. 3. 4.
G. Your Non-Assertive (Passive or Aggressive) behavior patterns Name one pattern	1. 2. 3. 4.	1. 2. 3. 4.

B. External Threats   (people, places, things, time, money issues, weather, etc.)

External Boundaries	Current Recovery Targets (behavior to stop doing)	Protection Plan/Steps (behavior to start doing)
Boundaries that Protect You from		
Dominating People (Demanding, controlling)	1. 2. 3. 4.	1. 2. 3. 4.
Spiritual Threats (Spiritual protection)	1. 2. 3. 4.	1. 2. 3. 4.
Financial Threats (Wasting your money)	1. 2. 3. 4.	1. 2. 3. 4.
Health Threats (Health decisions)	1. 2. 3. 4.	1. 2. 3. 4.
Interpersonal Threats (Toxic relationships)	1. 2. 3. 4.	1. 2. 3. 4.
Work Threats (Co-workers, boss, work load)	1. 2. 3. 4.	1. 2. 3. 4.
Time/Schedule Craziness (Things you put before God)	1. 2. 3. 4.	1. 2. 3. 4.

Lesson 11, Prayer Activity 5: Nailing Your "Lack of Protection Planning" to the Cross

Nothing changes inside of you until you ask God to change it. When you go to God and ask Him to help you in Jesus' name, He responds because He loves you and because you are His child. You must be willing to name the things in your flesh that are causing you and others pain and let Him take them, believing (faith in Him) that He can and will heal you. God does this because of Jesus' sacrifice on the cross, not because you (we) deserve it. None of us deserves God's mercy. It is a free gift to us paid for with great pain by Jesus.

Some of the main sources of mental and relationship pain come from growing up in dysfunctional families. Listed below are a few of the things that keep you trapped in pain identified in the "Setting Boundaries" lesson. Pray to God for those you want Him to take from you, for example:

- Lack of any consistent plan to protect myself from internal threats (my flesh)

- Lack of any consistent plan to protect myself from external threats (world, Satan)

- Understanding what my negative habitual behavior patterns are

- Identifying positive behavioral steps will create godly, healthy patterns

- Fear of asking for help from someone who can assist me in developing Boundaries that really work

Father God, I have struggled with_____ for many years, and it is causing me great pain. Please take it from me by washing my spirit clean from it. Please increase my faith in you, in the name of Jesus.

During the next week thank God every day for "washing your mind clean" even if your mind tells you it is still there or you feel like nothing has happened. This is your flesh trying to stay in control. Praise God ten times morning, noon and night for your healing. By your Faith you shall be healed. If you need more faith ask God for it.

Deep Healing: Lesson Twelve

Obedience is the Pathway to Your Purpose

The Light of Scripture:

Hebrews 5:7-9
During the days of Jesus' life on earth, he offered up prayers and petitions with loud cries and tears to the one who could save him from death, and he was heard because of his reverent submission. Although he was a son, he learned obedience from what he suffered and, once made perfect, he became the source of eternal salvation for all who obey him...

A Testimony to God's Deep Healing

For me, recovery was not just about stopping a behavior, but realizing and understanding the root cause of the behavior so that not only could I stop it but prevent it from recurring and relapsing into the same old patterns. Everett's class taught me concepts about human behavior (left brain vs. right brain wiring) and God's love and plan for my life. The first concept is to understand that I am highly valuable to God. I must value myself because Jesus died for me and God didn't send his Son to die for me because I'm worthless.

I have no right to self-criticism and self-accusations since the Holy Spirit is in me. I'm more valuable than diamonds because Jesus died for me. I must not treat myself as anything less. Nor does anyone else have a right to treat me as anything less. The concept of "we don't protect what we don't value" is critical to understand so that healthy boundaries can be established. No one else will protect me, my new boundaries enforce how I treat myself and how I will let other people treat me.

As boundaries were implemented and I "plugged in" with daily prayer, praise, and surrendering my will to God, I had fewer negative thoughts and my "self-worth" increased. My negative inner voice had allowed fear and worry to control me and I was critical of myself and others. It allowed me to dwell in blame, bitterness, regret over the past, and unforgiveness. This was a sin that required confession. Forgiving myself and others heals me. I learned that "if you blame you stay the same." I now understand that without forgiveness I cannot grow in the Lord.

I also learned that needs and desires make me selfish when they are not under God's control. I am responsible for ensuring my needs are met, but I now do so through God's Holy Spirit. No human can do that for me. Standing Firm (assertiveness) sometimes requires stepping out of my comfort zone, which can be a challenge for someone who was raised as the classic nice guy to always be polite, kind, and well mannered. I always wanted to please people rather than please God. I have learned to put God first and by doing so am now treating others better than I was before. I look forward to reading the book when it is finished as I have much more to learn if I am to serve God.   **Lance C.**

Fishing down in the Valley

You are in total awe as you watch your last big rock crashing through the thick brush down the steep mountain that caused you so much trouble.

Standing up, your guide smiles and says it is time to go and begins climbing back down the trail you had just come up.

Quickly standing up you ask him, "Where are you going…aren't we going to finish the climb? People will be able to see me better when I am on top of the mountain."

He stops and looks up at you on the ledge and says, "We didn't come to finish the climb, reaching the top of the mountain was never part of your purpose. We came this way to go as far as you needed to go to unload all of the rocks that were in your backpack. Now that you have done that you are ready to learn about your purpose. It is time to continue on with the next part of your journey."

Moving quickly to get off the ledge and back onto the trail you notice that your backpack is very lite. As you move back down the path you realize the journey is so much easier now than it was while carrying all those useless, self-destructive rocks. Your regret, remorse and shame are no longer there. For the first time in your life you feel a very strong sense of Hope that things can and will change for the better.

As you follow close behind your guide you ask, "So where do we go from here?"

"Down into the valley," he replied, "all of the people you need to help will always be down in a valley."

"What am I supposed to do when I meet them?"

He stops on top of a large mount waiting for you to catch up, looking down into the valley He answers, "Feed them nothing but the truth. Tell them how you are giving up your rocks. Tell them about your journey and most of all, tell them about me."

As he turns to continue down the path He motions with His hand towards the valley below, "Come, and follow me. Even though you walk through the valley you will not be alone. I will always be with you. I will never leave you nor forsake you."

Suddenly he faces you and with a big smile says, "You're really going to love fishing."

Descending into the valley you can hear many loud voices, actually cries of people who are suffering. Moving down the path faster with a new sense of urgency you suddenly recognize you are in the lead. His voice behind you guides you, "Always move towards the people, never move away from them. It pleases me when I see you caring for them with my love. That is your purpose. Go to them until I call you again. Stand firm doing your purpose until I come and get you for the rest of your journey."

Purifying Love

I worked my way through the university by working in the campus library. I was the night supervisor for six years and knew everyone who was employed in the four-story complex. Behind the main circulation desk worked a very kind lady named Bernice who was in her late 50s.

Unfortunately, Bernice was often sick. Her kidneys were failing so three times a week she had to receive dialysis treatments at the hospital.

Dialysis is the process of removing blood from a patient suffering from kidney failure, purifying it with a hemodialyzer (an artificial kidney) and immediately returning it to the person (body) from whom the blood was taken. The dialysis procedure performs all of the normal duties of the kidneys when the kidneys can no longer function by themselves; such as filtering out toxic waste products from the blood that will cause death.

What I find fascinating about dialysis is that the blood is circulated out of the body, cleaned of all the impurities in it and then put back into the body. So the blood itself is still useable, it is just the contamination in the blood that has to be removed.

Once the procedure is completed the person has the strength to return to daily living. The key for this process to work is that the patient must be willing to go through it as directed. The patients must submit (obey) to those who can help them in their weakness. They must trust the healing process if they are to survive.

The same is true for everyone who needs deep healing. You must trust and obey God's Word if you want the Holy Spirit to heal you. It is a purification process that brings you back to life so you do not perish from the poisons in your heart, mind, and relationships. This requires daily submission to God. If the healing process is to do what it is designed to do you must submit to God's commands for your life. Follow them and you can live with Jesus for eternity. Ignore them and you will die from the toxicity within your personality.

Healing Truth No. 61
Healing, recovery, and purification are all the same. You must purify your life if you are to recover your health, relationships and true identity.

The healing process is a "planned intervention" aimed at decontaminating your character so you can function as God created you to. Like dialysis, it filters out all of the bad character traits you have learned from the world and thankfully puts back in your godly ones. Participating in the healing process "when you feel like it" or "when you have time to" will only increase your illness and pain, not cure them.

Although the dialysis procedure was time consuming and expensive for Bernice she faithfully submitted because it meant life or death for her. Bernice "paid the price," because she valued her life and her time with her family. Doing the hard work of going to the hospital three times a week, and going through the long hours of discomfort bought her more time to be with the people she loved.

Spiritual Healing is the same. If you want to get healthy, improve your relationships with others, stop wasting your time and your money and spend the rest of eternity with Jesus then you must purify your soul by obeying God's commands. You must put in the hard work required if you want to survive the corruption operating within your flesh.

Spiritual Dialysis Brings Holiness through Purification

2 Corinthians 7:1
Since we have these promises, dear friends, let us purify ourselves from everything that contaminates body and spirit, perfecting holiness out of reverence for God.

When I first started my inner healing I thought it was impossible for me to ever be pure. How can anyone in this world be pure? It seems like an unachievable goal. But God taught me an important thing about purity: You are pure in His eyes only, if you are in Jesus and Jesus is in you.

It is Jesus who purifies you through the Holy Spirit. It is never based on good deeds that you do. For example, you can go to the hospital (church, workplace, home) every day with good intentions and help people who are in need but unless you hook up to God's "Holy Hemodialyzer" (Jesus' love through the Holy Spirit) the toxic impurities (sinful nature) stay within you. Bernice could not miss an appointment if she wanted to continue living and you cannot afford to miss God's mercy and grace if you want to live for eternity with Him. So how do you keep your appointment with God?

1. Submit: Bow down to Jesus daily and God the Father will set you free.

Isaiah 55:6
Seek the Lord while he may be found; call on him while he is near. Let the wicked forsake his way and the evil man his thoughts. Let him turn to the Lord, and he will have mercy on him, and to our God, for he will freely pardon.

2. Repent: Run towards God and away from sin.

Many people ask me to explain what "repent" means and I tell them it means "to run away from sin as fast as you can!" Repent means "to go in the opposite direction with great speed. Retreat, if you will, from whatever is destroying you."

Repenting involves much more than just stopping spiritually unhealthy behavior. As I previously stated you must not only stop the *bad* behavior but you must also replace it with *good* behavior. More importantly if healing and reconciliation are to take place so you can be restored you must pursue God's purpose for your life with as much speed as you use to run away from your sin. It is essential that you obey God's will for your life.

2 Timothy 2:22
Flee the evil desires of youth, and pursue righteousness, faith, love and peace, along with those who call on the Lord out of a pure heart.

So repenting (fleeing sin) could be defined as:

> "Pursuing God's will and purpose for your life with the same passion you used when you were filling your heart with selfishness, unforgiveness and immorality."

3. Purify: Ask God daily for the power of His Spirit to purify your mind

Romans 8:5-9
Those who live according to the sinful nature have their minds set on what that nature desires; but those who live in accordance with the Spirit have their minds set on what the Spirit desires.

The mind of sinful man is death, but the mind controlled by the Spirit is life and peace; the sinful mind is hostile to God. It does not submit to God's Truth, nor can it do so. Those controlled by the sinful nature cannot please God.

You, however, are controlled not by the sinful nature but by the Spirit, if the Spirit of God lives in you. And if anyone does not have the Spirit of Christ, he does not belong to Christ.

To be filled with God's Spirit (Holy Spirit, the Spirit of Christ) you must surrender your will, your mind, your heart and your life to God every day. We discussed "plugging in" early in the book. Learning scripture and obeying it in Jesus' name will set you free from your desires. All the internal lies and cravings that feed your self-destructive tendencies die within you. This is huge because when your desires connect with worldly temptations they sabotage you into doing self-destructive compulsive actions. These actions always seem right at the time but later prove to be fatal for your health, relationships, and future. When the Spirit of Christ lives in you, you have the power to obey God instead of your flesh (sinful nature).

Many Christians fall in temptation because they think they can mix the world's darkness with God's light. They never mention Jesus' commands or say anything about the evil controlling our world because they want others to like them. They live by fear and not by faith. But God will heal you and restore you to confess His name and deeds before others. You are called to expose evil and to help those who have fallen under its spell to find freedom.

Healing Truth No. 62
Fear nothing but God. Hate nothing but sin.

The following scripture was written thousands of years ago, but is one of the best descriptions of America and the world we live in today.

Psalm 12: 8
The wicked freely strut about when what is vile is honored among men.

Purity and obedience require you to fight against evil. You cannot be friends with the world and those who celebrate ungodly acts and expect to remain pure. Almost everything on TV now is anti-God, and impure in its stories and jokes but dying and going to hell is not a laughing matter. Your flesh wants to "party," but Jesus went in the opposite direction and denounced the flesh and world for its evil ways. If you are a citizen of heaven you automatically are at war with the world because it is at war with you.

1 Peter 2:11
Dear friends, I urge you, as aliens and strangers in the world, to abstain from sinful desires, which war against your soul.

4. Help People in Need. Serve God by helping (not fixing) others.

James 1:27
Religion that God our Father accepts as pure and faultless is this: to look after orphans and widows in their distress and to keep oneself from being polluted by the world.

An important part of inner healing is making the switch from "me, me, me" to putting others first. Self-centeredness and selfishness are key roots to all compulsive "acting out" behaviors. Trusting God to meet your needs will free you to share more of your energy by helping others in "appropriate" ways.

I say appropriate, because we are not helping others when we avoid taking responsibility for our own dysfunctional behavior patterns by supporting someone else's self- destructive behaviors. We cannot enable others to sin and call it helping; this is called codependency. Christians who are codependent believe they can earn salvation by "fixing" others when they have not yet let the Holy Spirit "fix" them.

Healing Truth No. 63
God doesn't want to make you happy He wants to make you *holy*. When you are holy you will be happier than you have ever been in your life because you will be blessed by God.

Luke 11:27-28
As Jesus was saying these things, a woman in the crowd called out, "Blessed is the mother who gave you birth and nursed you." He replied, "Blessed rather are those who hear the word of God and obey it."

The Good News is: Obedience Leads to Healing, Health, Holiness and Heaven.

Many people in life are happy but they are not holy. Happiness is not the pathway into heaven, holiness through Jesus Christ is.

1 Peter 1:22-23
Now that you have purified yourselves by obeying the truth so that you have sincere love for your brothers, love one another deeply, from the heart. For you have been born again, not of perishable seed, but of imperishable, through the living and enduring word of God.

God uses His Word like spiritual sandpaper to sand off the rough edges in your personality. This also strengthens your commitment to your purpose with challenging experiences that often expose self-defeating character flaws. King Saul rejected God's word and purpose leaving him impure, unholy and under control of his flesh, the world, and Satan. He rebelled against the Lord's will for his life and he paid for it with his life.

1 Samuel 15:22-23
Does the Lord delight in burnt offerings and sacrifices as much as in obeying the voice of the Lord? To obey is better than sacrifice, and to heed is better than the fat of rams. For rebellion is like the sin of divination and arrogance like the evil of idolatry, because you have rejected the word of the Lord, he has rejected you as king

Healing Truth No. 64
God isn't healing you so you can live separately from Him or others. He is healing you to be a stronger, more obedient, and loving servant of His.

So often we approach God as if He was an ATM machine and we need more money for more stuff. God's grace is not for us to keep and hoard. It is for us to share with others. He is calling all who need healing just like we do. When you give you will receive and the more you give the more you will receive. And the more you receive the more people God brings into your life to give to. In doing this you become more like Jesus who is giving you everything His Father in heaven gave Him.

Healing Truth No. 65
What you receive from God, He expects you to use to help others. The more you help others, the more He gives you. You can't keep what He gives you unless you give it away.

2 Corinthians 1:3-5
Praise be to the God and Father of our Lord Jesus Christ, the Father of compassion and the God of all comfort, who comforts us in all our troubles, so that we can comfort those in any trouble with the comfort we ourselves have received from God. For just as the sufferings of Christ flow over into our lives, so also through Christ our comfort overflows.

So What is Your (our) Purpose in This Life?

1. To love God and others by plugging-in to God's Love (Luke 10:27)

*Love the Lord your God with all your heart and with all your soul and with all your strength and with all your mind; and, love your neighbor **as yourself**.*

2. To Answer God's Call to Obedience (Romans 8:28)

And we know that in all things God works for the good of those who love him, who have been called according to his purpose. Our purpose is to fulfill His purpose.

3. To Walk in the Light by Telling the Truth and Confessing Sins (1 John 1:5-9)

This is the message we have heard from him and declare to you: God is light; in him there is no darkness at all. If we claim to have fellowship with him yet walk in the darkness, we lie and do not live by the truth. But if we walk in the light, as he is in the light, we have fellowship with one another, and the blood of Jesus, his Son, purifies us from all sin. If we claim to be without sin, we deceive ourselves and the truth is not in us. If we confess our sins, he is faithful and just and will forgive us our sins and purify us from all unrighteousness. If we claim we have not sinned, we make him out to be a liar and his word has no place in our lives.

4. To Live by Faith, not by Fear (2 Corinthians 4:16-17)

Therefore we do not lose heart. Though outwardly we are wasting away, yet inwardly we are being renewed day by day. For our light and momentary troubles are achieving for us an eternal glory that far outweighs them all. So we fix our eyes not on what is seen, but on what is unseen. For what is seen is temporary, but what is unseen is eternal.

5. Too Long to Be Clothed with Your Heavenly Dwelling (2 Corinthians 5:1-9)

*Now we know that if the earthly tent we live in is destroyed, we have a building from God, an eternal house in heaven, not built by human hands. Meanwhile we groan, **longing to be clothed with our heavenly dwelling,** because when we are clothed, we will not be found naked. For while we are in this tent, we groan and are burdened, because we do not wish to be unclothed but to **be clothed with our heavenly dwelling,** so that what is mortal may be swallowed up by life. Now it is God who has made us for this very purpose and has given us the Spirit as a deposit, guaranteeing what is to come.*

6. To Be Thoroughly Equipped and Prepared for Every Good Work (2 Timothy 3:17-4:2)

All Scripture is God-breathed and is useful for teaching, rebuking, correcting and training in righteousness, so that the man of God may be thoroughly equipped for every good work. In the presence of God and of Christ Jesus, who will judge the living and the dead, and in view of his appearing and his kingdom, I give you this charge: Preach the Word; be prepared in season and out of season; correct, rebuke and encourage—with great patience and careful instruction.

7. To Comfort Others in God's Spirit (2 Corinthians 1:3)

Praise be to the God and Father of our Lord Jesus Christ, the Father of compassion and the God of all comfort, who comforts us in all our troubles, so that we can comfort those in any trouble with the comfort we ourselves have received from God. "You Can't Keep it unless you Give it Away!"

8. To Feed God's Sheep (John 21:15-17)

When they had finished eating, Jesus said to Simon Peter, "Simon son of John, do you truly love me more than these?" "Yes, Lord," he said, "you know that I love you." Jesus said, "Feed my lambs." Again Jesus said, "Simon son of John, do you truly love me?" He answered, "Yes, Lord, you know that I love you." Jesus said, "Take care of my sheep." The third time he said to him, "Simon son of John, do you love me?" Peter was hurt because Jesus asked him the third time, "Do you love me?" He said, "Lord, you know all things; you know that I love you." Jesus said, "Feed my sheep."

9. To Go and Make Disciples (Matthew 28:18-20)

Then Jesus came to them and said, "All authority in heaven and on earth has been given to me. Therefore go and make disciples of all nations, baptizing them in the name of the Father and of the Son and of the Holy Spirit, and teaching them to obey everything I have commanded you. And surely I will be with you always, to the very end of the age."

10. Husbands, to Love Your Wives as Christ Loves You; Wives, to Respect Your Husbands (Ephesians 5:25, 28, 33)

Husbands, love your wives, just as Christ loved the church . . . In this same way, husbands ought to love their wives as their own bodies. He who loves his wife loves himself . . . However, each one of you also must love his wife as he loves himself, and the wife must respect her husband.

Lesson 12, Prayer Activity 1: List and Pray

Using the numbers provided previously, list down the three things above that you struggle with the most, as you work toward fulfilling your purpose. Pray over these three asking God to give you the power to complete them on a daily basis.

————   ————   ————

Lesson 12, Prayer Activity 2: Rating Your Effectiveness and Productivity
To be more effective and productive for Jesus, you must increase in His love.

2 Peter 1:5-8
*For this very reason, make every effort to add to your **faith** goodness; and to **goodness**, knowledge; and to **knowledge**, self-control; and to **self-control**, perseverance; and to **perseverance**, godliness; and to godliness, **brotherly kindness**; and to brotherly kindness, **love**. For if you possess these qualities in increasing measure, they will keep you from being ineffective and unproductive in your knowledge of our Lord Jesus Christ.*

Rate each gift:	Increasing in my life	Decreasing in my life
1. Faith		
2. Goodness		
3. Knowledge		
4. Self-control		
5. Perseverance		
6. Godliness		
7. Brotherly Kindness		
8. Love		

One Final Healing Truth
Obedience is the only pathway to God's purpose for your life.

To complete your spiritual purpose in this life, you not only have to walk the path God created for you, but you must also walk as He guides your feet to walk. You do this by letting God change something in you every day.

God isn't healing you to be happy; He is healing you to be Holy. By letting God (the act of obedience) move one foot in front of the other in each situation you encounter on the road to your purpose, you will become a blessing to Him, others, and yourself. Only He knows the way He wants you to go.

Psalm 119:105
Your word is a lamp to my feet And a light for my path.

Lesson 12, Prayer Activity 3: Developing an Attitude of Gratitude

Gratitude (thankfulness, appreciation, praise, and a high value for what one has or receives) must be based on God's Word rather than our perception of reality which is dominated by self-centeredness (your flesh, the world and you-know-who). When God's Holy Spirit is controlling our lives our perceptions are radically changed.

Example: "I use to hate being shoeless . . . until I met a man who had no feet."

Colossians 3:15-17
*Let the peace of Christ rule in your hearts, since as members of one body you were called to peace. And **be thankful**. Let the word of Christ dwell in you richly as you teach and admonish one another with all wisdom, and as you sing psalms, hymns and spiritual songs **with gratitude in your hearts** to God. And whatever you do, whether in word or deed, do it all **in the name of the Lord Jesus, giving thanks** to God the Father **through him**.*

What are three areas in your healing journey that you will praise God for helping you with?

1.

2.

3.

What are three things someone else said that really helped you focus on your healing process more?

1.

2.

3.

What are eight things you learned in this book (class) that you are grateful to God for teaching you, and that you will Praise Him for right now?

1.
2.
3.
4.
5.
6.
7.
8.

Lesson 12, Prayer Activity 4: Nailing Your Disobedience to the Cross

Some of the main sources of mental and relationship pain come from growing up in dysfunctional families. Listed below are a few of the things that can keep you trapped in pain as identified in the Obedience the Pathway to Your Purpose lesson. Pray to God about those you want Him to take from you, for example:

- Your defiant resistance to obey God's commands.

- Your refusal to learn God's Word, so you know His commands.

- The negative inner voice that tells you everything is OK as it is.

- Your lack of gratitude for all that God does for you every day.

- Confusion as to what your path in life should be.

- All the things that currently keep you from completing your purpose for God.

Father God, I have struggled with_____for many years, and it is causing me great pain. Please take it from me by washing my spirit clean from it. Please increase my faith in You, in the name of Jesus.

During the next week thank God every day for washing your mind clean even if your mind tells you something is still there, or you feel like nothing has happened. This is your flesh trying to stay in control. Praise God ten times morning, noon, and night for your healing. By your faith you shall be healed. If you need more faith ask God for it.

Power-Up Brothers and Sisters, Today You're Really Going to Need it!

1 Corinthians 1:18

For the message of the cross is foolishness to those who are perishing, but to us who are being saved it is the power of God.

ALSO BY

Everett T. Robinson

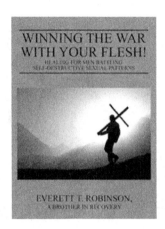

Winning the War with Your Flesh!

I have great respect for people who have gone through the worst of what life can throw at a person, and simply survive. I have even greater admiration for those who can turn around and help others make it, with the wisdom they've gleaned.

Everett Robinson is one of these rare individuals, a survivor and a survivalist of sexual addiction. You hold in your hand a manual that charts a course away from sexual temptation, flirtation, titillation, obsession and destruction. It puts feet to the Lord's prayer: "Lead us not into temptation, but deliver us from evil."

May you be delivered to a life of sexual wholeness and health. God bless you,

Dave Browning Senior Pastor, Christ the King Community Church, International Author of: Deliberate Simplicity, Hybrid Church and What Leaders Do.

Learn more at: www.outskirtspress.com/winthewar

CPSIA information can be obtained
at www.ICGtesting.com
Printed in the USA
FSOW03n0136250816
24142FS

9 781478 763178